THE COMPLETE BOOK OF
BITS & BITTING

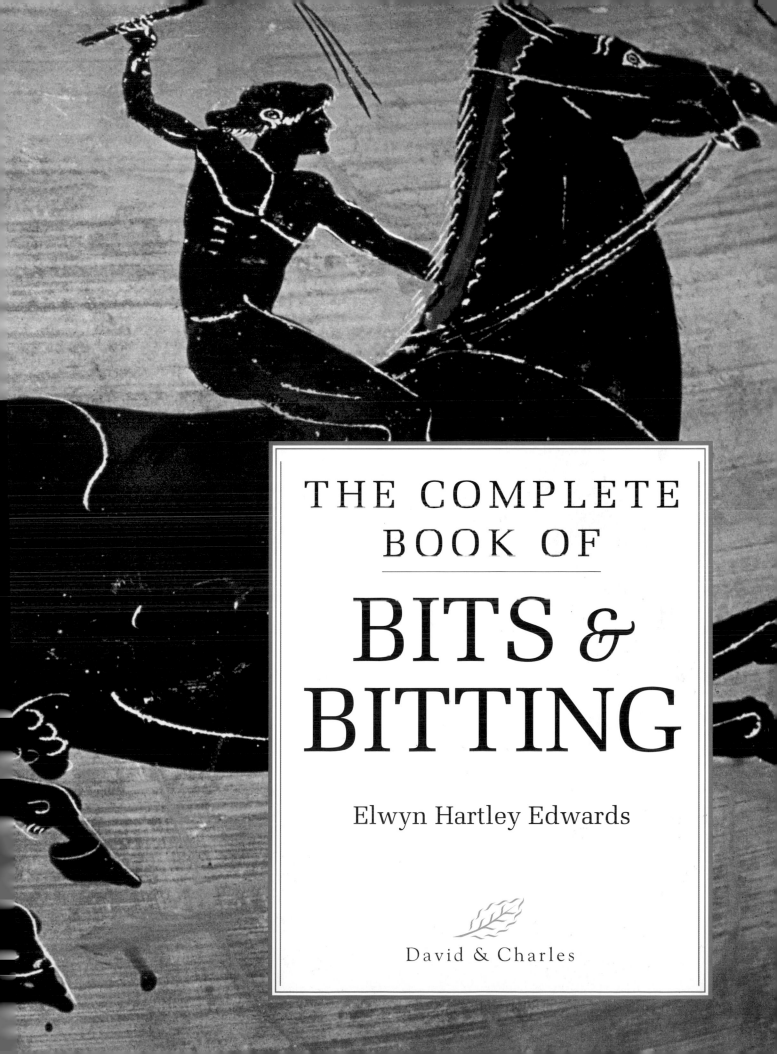

THE COMPLETE
BOOK OF
BITS &
BITTING

Elwyn Hartley Edwards

David & Charles

CONTENTS

INTRODUCTION

P rehistoric man would have been familiar with the herds of wild horses that moved southwards to escape the ice sheets of a million years ago. Later in time, 30,000 to 50,000 years past, our own ancestors, *Homo sapiens* – often referred to as Cro-Magnon man after the area in France where so much evidence of their existence has been found – hunted horses for food, as well as the bison, the wild ox and an assortment of other animals that shared their environment.

These people were responsible for the vivid cave art at places like Lascaux and Pech-Merle, art which was probably executed between 15,000 and 20,000 years ago. The paintings, still wondrous in their form and colour, represent one of the earliest forms of picturate communication and served to inform other hunters of the proximity of suitable quarry. Of course the relationship between man and the horses that were so frequently the subject of the Cro-Magnon artists, was that between the hunter and the hunted – but there was still an obvious sense of near-reverence for the animal so painstakingly depicted with colouring materials that have survived to our own time.

This vivid wall drawing in the caves at Lascaux, France, may have been executed 15,000 years ago. Probably, it represents a means of communication and indicates the presence of horses in the area to other groups of hunters

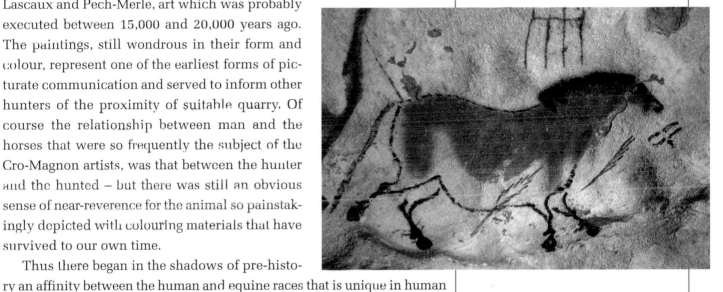

Thus there began in the shadows of pre-history an affinity between the human and equine races that is unique in human evolution and remarkable in its depth and intensity. In the millennia that followed the horse acquired an awesome stature. It became the symbol of power and majesty. Essential in life to the heroic image of their masters, the horses that bore the captains and the kings were often interred along with them in death. At various times and in many countries the horse, and particularly a white one, was revered as the ultimate, perfect sacrifice to the Gods, or, if he was lucky, was himself deified. Even today it is not unusual for the cortege of a great man to be followed by a charger carrying on his saddle the reversed boots of the deceased, and no great occasion of state is complete without its equine complement.

The watershed in the human/equine relationship and, consequently, in the history of the human race itself has to be the domestication of the animal species by the human. It is from that time that we can date the development of the means by which man was able to control an animal far bigger and stronger than himself, and as a result of that control, to co-opt the horse

in realising his restless ambitions and his potential to expand his influence, as a result of a superior intellect, over and within his environment.

We can also appreciate the truth in the saying: 'Man, encompassed by the elements which conspired to destroy him, by beasts faster and stronger than himself, would have been a slave, had not the horse made him a king.' That situation, which conferred a previously unimaginable mobility, was brought about by the creation of a control system based on the mouth, and so began the history of bitting. (The English word 'bit' derives from the Anglo-Saxon *bitan* – to bite.)

In the domestication charts the horse comes far behind the other animals. Dogs threw in their lot with man around or before 12000BC as a natural ally in the business of hunting. By 9000BC sheep, which like cattle are more tractable than horses, were kept in flocks, and cattle were 'enclosed' by pastoral peoples who had forsaken the nomadic lifestyle for that within a settled community.

In the next 2000 years goats, pigs and poultry were also added to the list of domestic animals, as well as the reindeer – and this is very important in the context of equine studies. The latter were certainly working in sledge harness in Northern Europe by 5000BC and may also have been

The use of reindeer in harness may date from 5000BC, about 1000 years before the domestication of the horse, and they may also have been ridden at that time. It is not unreasonable to suppose that the equipment of a reindeer culture provided a lead-in to that used by the early horse-peoples

systematically bred as well as ridden by that date. Without much doubt they had been 'herded', following the migratory pattern based on the growth of 'reindeer moss', throughout Outer Mongolia for probably 2000 years before.

The exact date of horse domestication is impossible to define but evidence points towards the end of the Neolithic period, between 4000 and 3000BC, and that it occurred in Eurasia, being accomplished by nomadic Aryan tribes moving in the steppe-lands bordering the Black and Caspian Seas – an area that in time was to be the very cockpit of the world.

It can be argued pretty convincingly that the first people to domesticate horses already had a tradition of reindeer herding, and they may also have been riders and drivers of those animals. The switch from reindeer to horse was facilitated by the increasing availability of the latter, and would have presented little difficulty to people familiar with the management of animals. Moreover because horses are not restricted to a migratory cycle,

they could be herded into grazing areas. And when grazing was covered by snow they were, by virtue of their strong single hoof, better equipped to forage for the food lying beneath.

The actual riding of horses as opposed to the herding of the animals for meat, milk, hides and so on, cannot have been long delayed. Clearly it would be more practical to direct a herd from the back of a horse than on foot, but it required some means of control.

Initially the 'bitting arrangement' may have been based loosely on a memory of the rough reindeer halter, and was probably nothing more than a thong tied round the nose. Nonetheless, the 'art of bitting' advanced

The Hittites, the first people to use the spoke-wheeled chariot in massed formation, had clearly evolved an effective bitting system to control their small but highly spirited horses

rapidly in the succeeding millennia as a matter of understandable urgency – after all, as the use of horses became more widespread the survival of an individual, a tribe or a nation was increasingly dependent on the ability to steer and stop an equine partner that, in relative terms, was becoming bigger, stronger and faster as the methods of horse management improved.

Not surprisingly, the early horseman – who, we must remember, rode without the security afforded by a saddle for over 3000 years and then waited another 600 to 700 years for the invention of the stirrup – placed great emphasis on the bit. Necessarily that pre-occupation was just as much shared by the chariot peoples, whose massed formations, operating on ideal flat and open country, dominated the rich valley lands of the Middle East for over 2000 years, and added a new dimension to warfare as the forerunner of the modern armoured division.

The Hittites who defeated the Egyptians at Kadesh in 1286BC, in what was the greatest chariot battle of antiquity, put no less than 3500

chariots into the field, each with its three-man crew and usually drawn by four horses, two harnessed to a central pole and two outriggers. Though small, these horses were clearly spirited, well conditioned and full of quality, if we are to believe the evidence provided by artefacts of the period. Effective bitting, in those circumstances, was an obvious priority in the interests of self-preservation, since the very natural concern of the horsemen of antiquity, whether they rode in the loose nomadic formations of the steppe horsemen or drove chariots in cohesive, well drilled divisions, was with the front end of their horses, where the head, and especially the mouth, provided the basis of control.

This was an attitude that persisted in the horsemanship of the Western world right into the Renaissance period, between the fifteenth and sixteenth centuries, and was not entirely absent in the military schools of Europe during the earlier part of the nineteenth century. Indeed the less charitable among us, witnessing a head carriage imposed by the hand without prior engagement of the quarters, might think that the bit still retained something of its old pre-eminence in equestrian circles today. Certainly the intricacies of bits and bridling

Right: By the eighteenth century, classical equitation had been developed as a rational science in which the careful bitting of the horse was a paramount requirement. This illustration by Johann Ridinger epitomises the light contact with the mouth which was the ultimate aim of the classical rider

Below: This picture of French riders schooling their perfectly balanced horses, the coloured horse performing one of the High School airs, admirably demonstrates control achieved by no more than the weight of a looped rein

have had a particular fascination for horse-people throughout the ages, and there have been periods in our history, most particularly in the seventeenth and eighteenth centuries, when the loriner's craft approached an art form in its own right. (A loriner is a maker of bits, stirrups and spurs.)

This book is itself an acknowledgement of the abiding and continuing interest in the subject felt by those who, though governed inexorably by high technology, still choose to be involved with the animal that has brought us to within sight of the millennium.

Nonetheless the bit, and, indeed, the whole subject of bitting, can be a two-edged sword unless there is a clear understanding of its role within the theory and practice of riding. It would be disastrous were we to think of the bit in isolation, and catastrophic were we to use it in that context.

The enormous range of bits and bitting auxiliaries can be both daunting and confusing, a difficulty that may sometimes be compounded by the claims made by largely uninformed manufacturers, and by notable gaps in national and international training syllabi.

Der Schluß auf einer halben Volte im Traverſirē das Pferd auf die Hancke geſetzt
Le Travers serré sur la demie Volte en mettant le cheval sur la hanche.
Nº28   J. E. R.

The prime purpose in the chapters that follow is to place the bit and its auxiliaries firmly into perspective as essential elements in the understanding of equitational theory. For this reason a chapter is devoted to the principles involved, which whilst viewing the bit and the hand within the combination of the 'aids', must necessarily include a study of the mouth itself and those parts of the head subjected to bit action.

I make no apology for the inclusion of the opening chapter tracing the history of the bit's development. It is, I believe, essential to our understanding not only of bitting but of the evolution of our present-day thinking about horses and riding.

E.H.E *Chwilog, 2000*

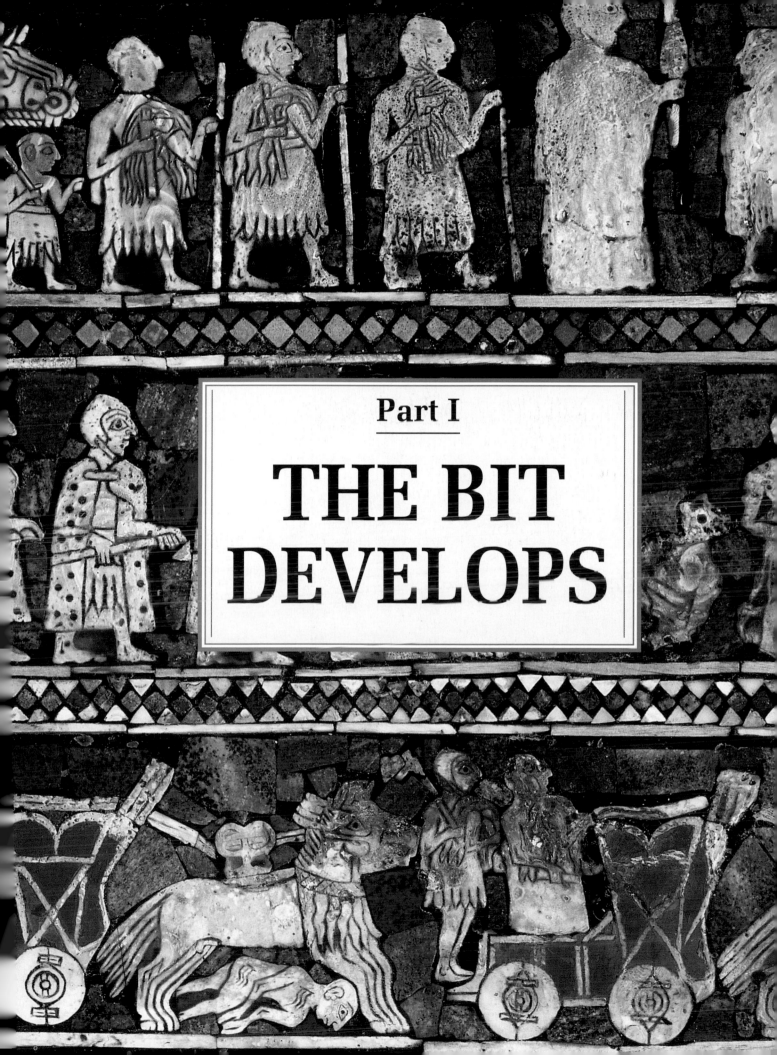

Part I

THE BIT DEVELOPS

THE HISTORY OF BITTING

It is reasonable to suppose that the first form of control practised by the early horsemen in the pre-Christian era relied upon nothing more than a simple halter made from woven grasses or from strips of leather. Probably it was much the same as the one used on reindeer, animals which had been ridden by the archetypal reindeer herders, the Uryanchai of Mongolia, for perhaps a millennium or more before the steppe tribes turned to the more versatile horse.

One imagines that it was only a short step from a halter, which would have followed the even more rudimentary neck rope, to a thong tied round the lower jaw between the molar and incisor teeth – across the 'bars of the mouth', in fact.

Both halter and jaw thong can be used with just a single rein passing to the hand on one or other side of the neck, and it is most likely that this was the case. A rein on the right side of the neck allows a turn to be made

Top right: Frank Remington's spirited Fantasy From the Pony Dance *shows the use of jaw thong, noseband and single rein by an accomplished natural horseman*

Bottom right: Remington's realistic portrayal of the travois pony is in direct contrast to the romantic depiction of the Indian chief on his war-horse, and the bitting arrangement is even more rudimentary, no more than a simple thong around the lower jaw

Below: Mongolian horsemen, displaying consummate skill, rely on the use of the neck-rein with a snaffle bit even when playing their fast and brutal war-games

in the same direction quite easily. It is a little more difficult, but by no means impossible, to turn to the left, when it is necessary to shift the weight to that side and apply the rein against the neck. The neck-rein closes the outside shoulder while opening the opposite one and compelling movement in that direction; moreover horses quickly learn to respond to its use. (Thousands of years later the serious, academic horseman had developed a system of rein effects – *see* p**46**. There are five of them, designed to allow the competent rider to position the horse with great precision. The fourth of those effects is called the 'indirect rein of opposition *in front* of the withers' and it moves the shoulders in one direction or the other according to which rein is applied. It is indeed a part of educated, rational horsemanship – but in essence it remains the neck-rein of the steppes and the desert lands!)

Five thousand years after the steppe tribes' domestication of the horse, the American Indian (now, in politically correct parlance, 'the native American') was riding, like his nomadic predecessors of Eurasia, with a thong round the horse's jaw;, interestingly, he also employed the *travois*, the horse-drawn

15

sled that had originated on the steppes. It is possible to argue a connection between the two peoples on the basis of some remarkable similarities in the two cultures, although that does not preclude the possibility of a nomadic Asian race finding its way over the northern landbridges which once connected the American continent with Asia to become, in the course of a millennium or two, the last of the world's horse-people – the American Indian.

Detail from the monumental Standard of Ur of the Chaldees shows onagers harnessed to solid-wheeled chariots and controlled from nose-rings

Oxen, which were in general use long before the horse, were directed by ropes attached to their horns, or, more effectively, were driven from a nose-ring; so too was the ill-tempered onager, whose employment also preceded that of the horse. The same method may have been applied to horses, but only in isolated circumstances and for a very limited period of time. (Sumerian artefacts of *c.*2500BC, in particular the monumental Standard of Ur of the Chaldees, depict solid-wheeled chariots drawn by onager teams whose reins were attached to nose-rings, or rings passed through the upper lip, and kept in position by a strap fastening under the jaw.)

In the centuries preceding and following the Christian era, Numidian

horsemen of North Africa seem to have managed pretty well without any sort of bridling arrangement. They controlled their horses, as we are told by that meticulous observer, Silius Italicus, by 'plying a light switch between their horses' ears'. Donkeys in North Africa are ridden in just the same manner to this day. But that would not do at all in the case of a war-chariot driven at break-neck speed with a team of four spirited horses.

The halter and the thong quickly gave way to a bit, held in place by a headpiece and often supported by a low-fitting noseband. These first bits were straight bars made first from hardwood and then from bone and horn. Such bits were in use *c.*2300BC, about the time when the onager was phased out, and between 1300 and 1200BC metal bits, of bronze, were in general use throughout the Near East, although they had appeared in various of the horse tribes well before that date.

Almost from the outset horsemen seem to have appreciated the increased severity of a jointed bit exerting a nutcracker action over the lower jaw. Although the straight-bar mouthpiece never became obsolete, the jointed bit found increasing favour with the nomadic horsemen of Eurasia and also with the chariot-people of the flat valley lands of the Middle East.

The mouthpieces were made more powerful in their action by the addition of spikes, serrated edges and the like, and in the case of the chariot could be supported by the rein passing downward from the bit through rings set low on the harness pad before coming into the hand.

Standard of Ur of the Chaldees (c.2500BC). The ill-tempered, but more widely available onager, preceded the use of the horse in the war chariot

The resultant sharp angle increased immeasurably the restraint that could be exerted on the mouth.

Lateral control might be accentuated by cheeks or rings fitted with sharp burrs that pricked into the sides of the face. Their twentieth and twenty-first century counterparts are not much different, and when one sees the modern racehorse wearing today's equivalent of the notorious ring bit used by North African horsemen who acted as cavalry *foederati* to the Roman legions, one realises that there has been little significant advance in bit design since the Celts of Gaul introduced the curb bit in the fourth century BC!

Nonetheless, although the ancient world was aware of the curb bit – it was certainly known to the horsemen of classical Greece, for instance – early equestrian thinking was dominated by the snaffle, a situation that was to pertain up to the Middle Ages. Indeed, the horsemen of Central Asia – the Mongols, Tartars and Huns – never did forsake it, for the snaffle exactly suited the forward-style of riding adopted by these superlative horse-archers; they rode with shortened leathers in a very modern cross-country seat centuries before an American jockey, Tod Sloan (1874–1933) adopted the forward crouch that revolutionised race riding, or Federico Caprilli (1868–1907) made the shortened leather central to the Italian *sistema*,

Left: Assyrian cavalry (ninth century BC) riding fast and in close formation – a tribute to their horsemanship and the bitting method employed

which became known as the 'forward seat'. Later, the Hungarian hussars, the *beau ideal* of the dashing, swift-moving light horseman, were cast in the same mould, eschewing entirely any suggestion of collection which they associated with the Renaissance schools and which they regarded as impossibly restrictive.

CAPTAINS AND RULERS

The most informative visual evidence of early bitting developments is provided by Assyrian artefacts between the ninth and sixth centuries BC, before the Assyrians gave way to the Persians as the foremost 'world power'.

But before them, there are Egyptian reliefs and tomb paintings that show fiery horses driven to chariots and obviously effectively bridled. One of the first records of a man sitting on an obviously spirited

Above: Relief from the North Palace at Ninevah. Following the reigns of the Assyrian Kings, Assurbanipul (885–860BC) and Shalmaneser III (859–824BC) the Assyrian archers are shown as confident, aggressive horsemen. The rein of the elaborate and sophisticated bridle may have been secured to a hook fitted above the wither

Left: Tomb of Nebamun, Thebes, c.1400BC. These strong chariot horses are controlled by a rein passing from the mouth through a ring on the driving pad that allows greatly increased leverage against the mouth

horse appears on a relief decorating the tomb of Horenhab of Egypt. It is dated at about 1600BC and the rider is sitting on the animal's rump in the way that men, right up to the present time, sit on an ass. He controls his horse from a strong noseband fitted low on the nose, for all the world like the modern drop noseband. Possibly, too, there may have been 'straps' crossing over the face. These in themselves constitute a form of restraint, though the effect is psychological rather than physical.

Those crinkle-bearded, richly caparisoned warriors, the Assyrians – 'Captains and rulers clothed

most gorgeously, horsemen riding upon horses, all of them desirable young men' – were the same horsemen who caused anxiety to the prophet Ezekiel on account of their attentions to the not unwilling daughters of Israel. More objectively they were undisputed masters for some 300 years of the lands about the Tigris and Euphrates and from the Persian Gulf westwards towards Egypt and north to Luristan and Kurdistan.

Initially the Assyrians were chariot-people, and in the days of Assurbanipal (885–860BC) and into the reign of Shalmanesar III (859–824BC) depictions of their mounted warriors reveal some very apprehensive-looking horsemen led by attendants. Their chariots, on the other hand, give quite a different impression – strong, immaculately groomed stallions and stern, obviously capable fighting men armed with bows and javelins.

But by the reign of Tiglath-Pileser III (747–727BC) the Assyrian cavalry present quite a different picture. Here are confident, armoured riders, spearmen and archers sitting on richly embroidered saddle-cloths and riding active, well made horses that are immaculately coiffured and wear ornate and sophisticated bridles.

The bit is a jointed snaffle, the mouthpiece probably studded with blunt spikes, and the cheeks are in the shape of a triangle with the base crescent shaped. It is kept in place by an elaborate headpiece that usually incorporates straps crossing high on the face. The horses, which are stallions, are depicted with powerful, arched necks but with the face always held in advance of the vertical. Nonetheless, the bridle is a powerful means of restraint, and its construction, allowing that the bit is a snaffle acting somewhat upwards against the lips, must also ensure some downward pressure on the poll as well as a secondary pressure on the face at the juncture of the two straps. However, this latter is too high to induce any significant retraction of the nose. There is some evidence to suggest that the bit itself might have been attached to a noseband, or that a noseband independent of the bit was fitted below it in the mode of our familiar drop noseband; in particular this was true of chariot horses. If that were so, the measure of control would be increased substantially.

The see-saw in the struggle for the great Near Eastern civilisation witnessed the decline of the Assyrians by the sixth century BC, in the face of the increasing expansion of the Persian Empire.

Above: Assyrian cheek snaffle with a central ring that is surprisingly modern in appearance. It was secured in the mouth by thongs passed through the holes above and below the mouthpiece

Right: Elaborate bronze cheek-pieces from Persian bits 700–500BC. Decoration has been a feature of horse equipment from the time of the first horse-peoples

Below: Another and even more elaborate bronze cheek-piece from Western Persia 900–700BC that indicates the high standing of the horse in early civilisations

PERSIA AND THE SUPER-HORSE

As big a factor as any in the development of bitting up to the twentieth century was the development of the horse itself. As it became more and more selectively bred, and was increasingly the object of improved methods of management, with access to more nutritious feedstuffs, the horse grew bigger and stronger, matters which, inevitably, posed additional problems of control – particularly for horsemen still riding on a cloth and without the security endowed by a stirrup. It was easier, of course, for the charioteer, who could brace himself against the front boards of his vehicle and use his weight on the reins.

By the third century BC the Persian Empire stretched from Egypt to Asia Minor and from India to the Greek Islands, largely as a result of the Persians gaining control of the Great Silk Road route and the adjacent lands of ancient Media, which gave access to the breeding grounds of the renowned Nisean horse.

Raised over a period of some 1500 years in the cool foothill pastures, and well conditioned on the high-protein alfalfa crops, it was heavier in build than the horses of the Assyrians, the Hyksos and the horse-peoples who had gone before. It was also a coarser, less refined animal, but it was hard and strong, possibly on account of infusions of the blood of

Below: Castaigne's ferocious depiction of the charge of the Persian scythe chariots. 'The armoured Persian horsemen and the death-dealing chariots were invincible. No man dared face them'

the Mongolian or Asiatic Wild Horse (*equus caballus Przewalski Przewalski Poliakov*).

Herodotus gives a chilling description of the Persian armies: 'The armoured Persian horsemen and the death-dealing chariots were invincible,' he wrote, 'no man dared face them.'

To be invincible, or even effective, it is imperative that cavalry and chariot formations act cohesively and remain subject to the control of the commanders, a fundamental requirement that at various times in the history of warfare was neglected by the mounted arm. In simplistic terms it implies that horsemen, mounted or driving chariots, must be capable of exerting a modicum of control over their animals, even in the heat of battle, and that could have posed a problem for men riding horses of the calibre of the Nisean.

The Persian bit may not have varied too much in its action or design from that used by the Assyrians, other than the phallus-shaped cheek often being decorated with the shape of a horse's hoof. (Both are symbolic of the stallion's fertility and in a modified form can be seen today in the 'horseshoe' cheek bits worn with a stallion bridle.)

Interestingly, and for the first time in the history of the ridden horse, the thick-necked Persian horses are depicted with the head held in what amounts to an 'overbent' position, with the chin tucked in to the chest. Nosebands above and below the bit, and straps crossing the face diagonally with some running upwards centrally from the bit rings are noticeable features of the elaborate Persian bridles, and it is reasonable to assume that they were responsible for the positioning of the head and thus the increase in control afforded to the rider.

In many instances the noseband is fitted directly to the bit and would thus act in concert with the latter. Furthermore, it is more than a probability that the nosebands were fitted with spikes or burrs on the inside surface, an arrangement that exerts an obviously powerful restraint.

The form of bridle used today by the *gaucho* of South America and the Ukrainian Cossack can be seen clearly as echoing the Persian pattern, whilst the 'spiked' noseband is still in evidence as the Iberian *careta* and was in use in the classical schools of the Renaissance and, long before that, in the sub-continent of India.

A gaucho bridle from South America that would not have looked out of place on a Persian war-horse

THE FIRST MASTER

The age of classical Greece is considered to have begun in 480–479BC after the repulse of the first attempted invasion by the Persians, whose empire disintegrated after the conclusive defeat of Darius by Alexander the Great

at Issus in 333BC. The Greeks were not horsemen in the mould of the Scythians, Huns and Mongols, but horses played a central role in Greek life, the élite of Greek society belonging to the knightly 'equestrian' class.

The first manuals of horse training that we know of were those of Kikkuli the Mittanian, written in about 1360BC. Much later a Greek, Simon of Athens, produced an instructional manual for chariot horses, but the works that have survived most completely are those written by the Greek cavalry commander, Xenophon (430–356BC), and they exerted an influence that has extended, remarkably, into our own time.

Xenophon was a man of many parts. He was at once an historian, agriculturalist and philosopher in the mould of Socrates his teacher, as well as being a prominent military commander. His achievement was to leave the world a legacy of horsemanship as an art. It was he who provided the inspiration for the enquiring horsemen of the Renaissance and a base for what we now term classical riding. Throughout, books like *Hippike*, *Hipparchikos*, *Anabasis* (The Retreat of the Ten Thousand from Persia,

Alexander the Great (356–323BC), the most outstanding military figure of antiquity. Alexander, the victor of Issus, was himself a notable horseman and a cavalry commander of genius

when the Greek army was saved by his leadership), *The Cavalry Commander* and *The Art of Horsemanship* there runs a strong element of humanity, an unusual quality to find among the horsemen of antiquity and one noticeably absent in their successors up to perhaps the twentieth century.

Xenophon's training manuals are comprehensive and surprisingly modern in their content. Horses are schooled to strike off on the correct leg at canter; much emphasis is given to work on the circle as a suppling and balancing exercise, and the demi-pirouette from canter was included in the training programme. Horses were taught to jump across country, and the selected 'parade' horses performed the equivalent of the modern passage as a matter of course. Furthermore they were schooled in the levade, the High School half-rear executed with flexed hocks, the horse sinking on his haunches while raising the forehand and tucking up the forelegs: 'The prettiest feat a horse can do' wrote Xenophon.

The carefully structured training and conditioning programmes reveal also a deep understanding of horse psychology; moreover they are all the more remarkable since the Greek horsemen rode without saddles and, in the heroic tradition of classical nudity, usually without breeches, too, although in battle they wore armour. Naturally, under the circumstances, great emphasis was given to the bit, and Xenophon's writings represent the first, serious study of bit construction in relation to the horse's mouth and the use of the bit within the spectrum of effective horsemanship. (Greek horsemen also understood the use of the leg and were accustomed to using a short 'prick' spur.)

The Greek bits, all of them very modern in appearance, were snaffles, with and without cheeks and with carefully graded, jointed mouthpieces designed to suit a variety of horses. The mouthpiece was fitted with spike or studded rollers, *icheni* – literally 'seahorses' – which could be small and blunt or by degrees larger and sharper.

Bits for young horses had smooth rollers set round the mouthpiece, or were fitted with small lengths of chain like the modern 'keys' in a present-day breaking snaffle. Xenophon writes of the young horse 'pursuing the bit with his tongue'.

The soft bit was always preferred to severe ones, and continual emphasis was given to the desirability of a light, sympathetic hand. 'It is not the bit,' wrote Xenophon, 'but its use that results in a horse showing its pleasure so that it yields to the hand; there is no need for harsh measures; he should rather be coaxed on so that he will go forward most cheerfully in his swift paces.'

Left: Xenophon (430–356BC), a student of Socrates, was a soldier, historian and agriculturalist and is regarded as the first Master of equitation

Greek bit of 400–300BC, fitted with icheni. The mouthpiece is severe but Xenophon's preference was for the 'soft' bit rather than a severe one

The quotation would not be out of place if it were written large on the walls of modern riding schools, and there are others, just as apposite, that illustrate the approach to horses taken by the Greeks and the recognition of the necessity to understand the equine mentality. 'What is done by compulsion is done without understanding and there is no more beauty than in whipping or spurring a dancer.'

Nonetheless, the Greek bridle frequently incorporated the *psalion*, a metal cavesson acting on the nose, a device which in one form or another had been in use for a thousand years previously. This recognition of nose pressure to support the bit and the employment of nosebands that would act powerfully to restrain an impetuous animal persisted into and past the period of the classical Renaissance schools. Indeed, it was central to the system of training well into the seventeenth and eighteenth centuries. Today, the Iberian horseman still uses the studded *careta*, and of course nose pressure is integral to the training of the Western horse, the Californian reinsman having inherited his techniques from the sixteenth-century *conquistadores*.

The Greek horse was more oriental in character than the coarser Persian animals, and despite the influence of the *psalion* they carried their heads

The great Frieze of Parthenon says everything about the heroic image of Ancient Greece and not a little about the natural skill of the Greek horseman

closer to the horizontal plane, if we are to believe the evidence of numerous statuary and reliefs. The Parthenon frieze is an example in point.

After the death of Alexander the Great in 323BC Greece reverted to a loose confederation of states, but the Greek legacy to the world – our modern democracies, for example – was far from exhausted. In the equestrian world the Greek influence would be felt again by the horsemen of the Renaissance as they re-discovered Xenophon's works. It was not until the sixteenth century that a book on horsemanship that could be compared with Xenophon's works made its appearance. Classical Greece and Rome exerted a continuing influence on the affairs of mankind, bequeathing to the world the advantages of a rational system of order and the legacy of democratic government.

The contribution of the supremely literate Xenophon to the advance of horsemastership was similarly of historic proportion. It included a study of bitting, and indeed it attempted, not unsuccessfully, to put the bit itself into perspective within the overall context of riding. When the Roman Empire finally succumbed to the onslaught of the 'barbaric' (ie non-Greek and non-Roman) horsemen in the fourth century AD the world, including that of the horse, entered into the Dark Ages.

A utilitarian snaffle of the Iron Age, first century AD, with a fixed ring which would imply a forcible use of the hand to bring the mouthpiece into play

ROME, CELTS AND CURBS

The Romans were reluctant horsemen but they were vigorous in the promotion of horse-breeding to produce stock for every purpose, from common draught to the prancing, snorting *cantherius* carrying an emperor in his triumph. Militarily, they put their trust in a large, effective navy and the impenetrable shield-wall of their superbly drilled legions. To support the latter, they employed the *alae* to cover the wings of the army. These were made up from foreign, mercenary horsemen and it was through them that further developments in bitting were introduced.

This Celtic bronze bit of the same period is for a chariot horse, the inside ring, with a single boss, provided the rein attachment to the pair horse. In comparison to the iron bit it is a work of art

Indeed, the contribution of the Celts marks an important stage in equestrian practice. The Celts, as well as being formidable warriors, were clever, inventive people who were the iron-workers of the ancient world and appreciated as such by the pragmatic Romans. They were responsible for the invention of the horseshoe and it was they who introduced another dimension in horse-control with the curb bit, a concept which became almost central to the later use of Rome's armoured *catafracti*, the heavy cavalry that could be launched in close formation to break bodies of foot soldiers. For the nomadic, swiftly moving horsemen of central Asia the philosophy of heavy cavalry was virtually an alien concept, and so, in consequence, was the curb bit. They stuck to the snaffle which suited their hit-and-run guerrilla tactic admirably, and complemented their

inherent skill as the world's foremost horse-archers. (Rome, too, had its light cavalry, the *clibanarii*, formed of barbarian horsemen, but though their purpose was to provide a swiftly-moving flank guard for the legions as well as to harass, pursue and reconnoitre, they acted cohesively under the firm hand of Roman commanders.)

Nonetheless, outside of the steppe-lands, it was the curb bit that would increasingly dominate both the battlefield and equestrian thought and practice, and this would be for the best part of 1500 years after Attila the Hun, in 451, crushed forever the steadfast legions at the Catalaunian Fields. The Roman curb bits were surprisingly advanced in design, even employing a ported mouthpiece, but they did not complete the system of levers by the addition of a curb chain — that came a little later and may not have been in general use until the latter part of the Middle Ages.

Among the Roman cavalry *foederati* were substantial detachments of Numidians from North Africa as well as the mysterious 'X' group, known to the Romans as the Nobades. These latter were probably Negroid, but though their burial mounds are to be found in Nubia, along the present Egyptian-Sudanese

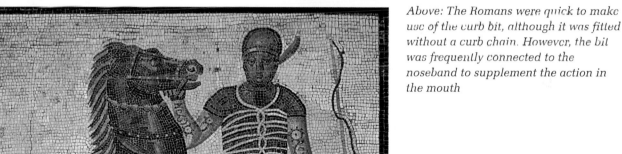

Above: The Romans were quick to make use of the curb bit, although it was fitted without a curb chain. However, the bit was frequently connected to the noseband to supplement the action in the mouth

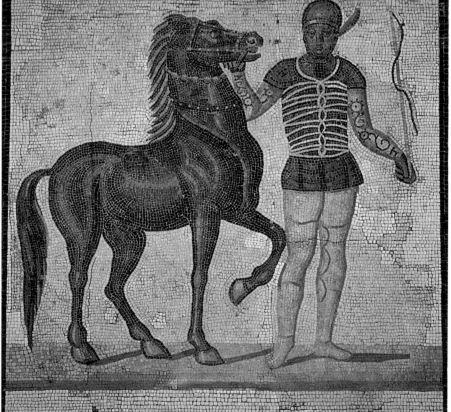

Left: The bit on this Roman chariot horse is almost certainly attached to a tightly fitting noseband

border, their precise origin remains unknown to this day.

What we do know is that they rode oriental or Arab-type horses using a boat-shaped saddle built on a tree, but without stirrups. They used a long lance underhand, rather than in the more usual overhand, stabbing manner of the time, and like the Sarmatians, steppe tribes of Iranian stock, they rode home in the shock tactic of the charge. What is of great interest in the context of the bit is that they used a unique form of ring bit made from iron and sometimes from silver: this encircled the jaw, and in the hands of the uninitiated it had the potential to snap the jaw-bones like a rotten twig. The Mamelukes, an elite group of slave soldiers originating in central Asia and active in Egypt and North Africa between the thirteenth and early nineteenth centuries, used a more elaborate, 'improved' version of the ring bit, but which was just as lethal in its effect.

Since it would have been hardly feasible to employ large detachments of horses suffering from broken jaws, one is bound to conclude that the Nobades, Mamelukes and all were exceptional horsemen, able to ride in formation at speed and control their horses on a more or less looping rein.

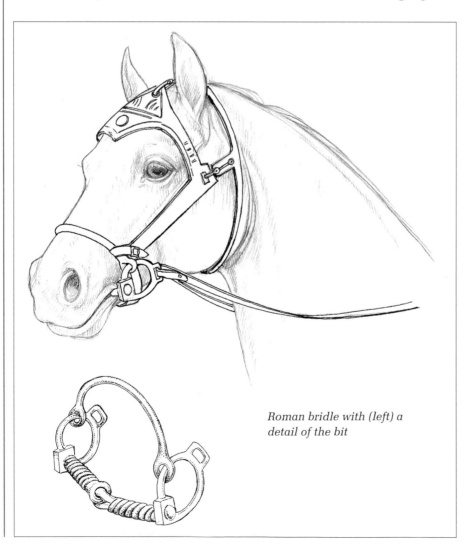

Roman bridle with (left) a detail of the bit

THE MIDDLE AGES

For convenience we can take the Middle Ages as beginning in 1066 when
William the Conqueror invaded England. The date may be a simplifica-
tion, but from that point we can trace the development of civilisation and,
of course, of bitting from a plethora of pictures, artefacts and written
records. What went on before, in the Dark Ages, is pretty well unknown.

For a century or more there is still evidence of the snaffle being used
by horsemen clad in chain mail and the like, and the Bayeux tapestry
shows Norman knights using snaffle or snaffle-type bits; but as horses get
bigger and the knights, as well as their mounts, are ever more heavily
armoured, the curb bit, increasingly horrendous in its proportions, comes
into general use. In some instances the cheeks on these fearsome bits were
up to 22in (55cm) long, and the possible leverage that could be applied
to the poll and lower jaw was commensurably severe – *if, that is, the bit
was ever used in so forceful a manner.*

In fact, everything points to the medieval horseman being a skilled and
accomplished rider and his horse a highly trained one. The medieval knight
had the advantage of a secure seat by virtue of his deep-seated saddle, built
high at front and rear, and also, of course, by the possession of a stirrup.

He rode long, leg outstretched to the front and body braced against the
rear of the saddle, in which position he was less likely to be unseated at
the moment of impact with enemy infantry, or to be flung dangerously forwards on the high pommel of his saddle should the horse stumble or fall.

*The Bayeux tapestry shows William's
Norman Knights at the Battle of
Hastings (1066) using relatively simple
snaffle-type bridles*

*Top left: The bit of the Emperor
Constantine the Great (274–337). He
converted to Christianity in 312 and
this bit is reputed to have been forged
from nails taken from the Holy Cross*

*Centre left: The notorious ring bit of
North Africa. It was the bit of the
Mamelukes and the Nobades, both
exceptional horsemen*

*Below left: A Roman curb of advanced
design and excellent workmanship
fitted with rollers round the mouthpiece
but not employing a curb chain*

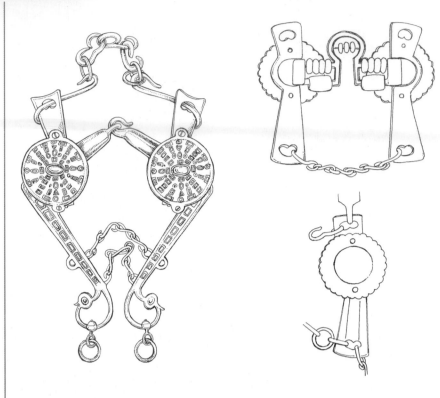

Far left: This ornate curb bit made for Louis XI of France is part of the treasure of Bourges Cathedral. It is made of bronze, extravagantly gilded, enamelled and jewelled

Left: An intricate French curb bit of the 14th century. The complexity of the arrangement of rollers is remarkable and unusual; below, detail of the cheek

Below: A German bit of the late 15th century. The mouthpiece is simple when compared with the French bit but the cheek measures 32cm (16ins)

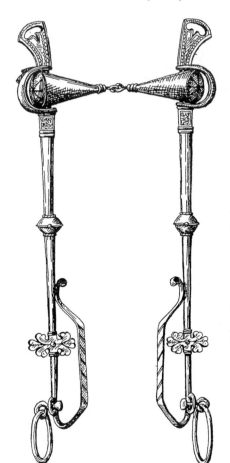

A further reason for carrying the leg so far to the front was the position of the stirrup. The stirrup leather was, indeed, attached so far to the front of the saddle that it would have been difficult to have sat otherwise. It was also the leg position that made it necessary to employ very long-shanked spurs if they were to reach the horse's flanks.

There is little doubt that the knight had learnt how to control his horse's quarters with leg and spur, and to do so with some effect. As for the bit, that had to be operated with one hand, namely the left one: this held the rein and also the long, triangular shield, and the latter compelled the rein-hand to be held at chest height. The right hand bore the sword, lance or mace.

The very valuable horses would have been schooled to the neck-rein aid as well as made responsive to the spur, while the bridle hand needed only to be raised when restraint was necessary, because with a bit of that potential severity, just the threat of more coercive action was sufficient to control the horse. They rode, indeed, by the *threat* of a severe bit rather than by its application. Their successors of the classical schools of the Renaissance did the same thing, and so does the Iberian horseman and the Californian reinsman of today.

It is sometimes disputed whether the classical 'airs above the ground', demonstrated today at Vienna's Spanish Riding School and at Saumur by France's Cadre Noir, originated in the movements practised by the medieval knight in 'press of battle'. Probably they are best regarded as a supreme refinement of a medieval ideal but, up to the time when the war-horse became impossibly heavy and over-burdened, there

Right: Increasingly the knights of the Middle Ages controlled their heavy mounts with long-cheek curb bits, the rein being held in the left hand

is no reason to suppose that schooled horses were not taught to kick out behind to discourage the attentions of foot soldiers or to perform the half-rear of the levade. Quite certainly, a half-pirouette to either hand would have been a necessary accomplishment to allow the use of the sword arm through 180°.

In common with many men of action as well as a whole progression of horsemen through the ages, the medieval knight was no great shakes with a pen, and so much of the training involved falls within the area of conjecture, albeit a fruitful one. Nonetheless, his was an inevitable and powerful influence upon the continuing development of riding, along with the traditions of Byzantine horsemanship which were necessarily at the very root of training for the battlefield and the tournament.

THE ERA OF CLASSICISM

Without doubt the cradle of classical riding was formed by the schools of horsemanship that flourished in Naples during the Renaissance. Federico Grisone, accepted as the first of the classical masters of the period, founded his school there in 1532. His teaching derived from that of Xenophon, which had influenced the horsemen of Byzantium, and

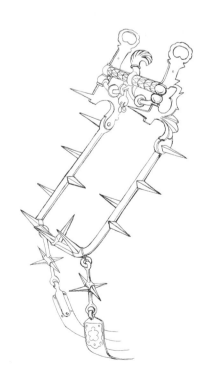

Above: Capriole in hand as performed at France's Cadre Noir. The High School 'leaps' or 'airs above the ground' had their foundation in the early Byzantine schools

Above left: The capriole *(the leap of the goat) performed under saddle*

Left: This fearsome-looking fifteenth-century bit was spiked to discourage the enemy during hand-to-hand fighting

very particularly from the practice of the Byzantine circus. In fact a Byzantine school had been established in Naples some four hundred years before, in 1134.

Grisone used some very severe bits and invented many more, some of horrific complexity. A man of his time, Grisone's methods were barbaric by the standards of the twentieth century, although he schooled on the system of reward and correction which had been initiated by Xenophon. The emphasis, however, was more on correction than otherwise, reward amounting to not much more than a cessation of punishment. But Grisone also insisted on preserving the lightness and sensitivity of the mouth. For him and the classical masters who were to expand riding into an art form, extreme lightness of hand within supreme collection was the ideal, a sort of Holy Grail to be pursued with unswerving purpose.

It is this philosophy of contact by the weight of a looping rein, maintained throughout the most advanced movements, that marks the divide between true classic *art* and the modern twang-taut contact between hand and mouth that too often characterises the *sport* of modern dressage.

To obtain lightness the classical masters, right up to the greatest of them all, François Robichon de la Guérinière (1688–1751), made much

33

use of the 'false rein' attached to rings of a metal-nosed cavesson, the studded noseband of antiquity. The horse was, indeed, literally 'mouthed' through the nose, control passing gradually from the false rein to the threat of the powerful curb bit.

A variation on the 'false rein' was Newcastle's 'running rein', in reality a more sophisticated retractive force to flex the poll so that the face was carried in the vertical plane. William Cavendish, Duke of Newcastle (1592–1676) is acknowledged as the sole English master and his work was both recognised and admired by Guérinière himself. His rein fastened at the girth and came to the hand through the side rings of the cavesson, and it was probably more effective than the conventional 'false rein'.

Of course, there were cavessons of unacceptable severity. Thomas Blundeville (1565) condemned the use of a fierce chain noseband, derived from the Moorish practice, as being too severe, 'for that it straineth the tender gristle of his nose too sore'. Then there was the *musrole*, made of twisted iron, which was too much even for Grisone. He considered it entirely non-productive, causing the nose 'by its violence ... to arise in the middle like the beak of a hawk'.

William Cavendish, Duke of Newcastle, the sole British Master, performing the ballotade *on the classical looped rein contact*

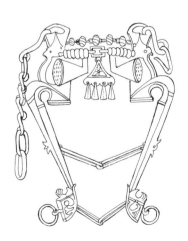

A bit of 'horrific complexity' designed by Federico Grisone who founded his school of horsemanship in Naples in 1532

34

After the 'false rein', or perhaps side by side with it, came the 'flying trench', an addition attached above the mouthpiece which was the forerunner of the bradoon now employed with the double bridle. Sometimes, too, a top rein would be fastened to the top loop of the curb, after the fashion of a Pelham.

Having regard to the generally heavy and common horses which were available, it is not surprising that the early classicism relied greatly upon coercion applied at both ends. To perform the balanced airs of the manège, let alone the 'airs above the ground', collection was obtained from a severe bit in front (or, in fairness, to the threat of it in the case of Grisone), and the whip and spur applied energetically to engage the quarters behind. Frequently, the whips (and worse) were laid on from behind by dismounted assistants.

The principle of bringing both ends towards the middle, shortening the outline and encouraging the engagement of the quarters, remains with us today, though thankfully in a more refined form. Two hundred years after

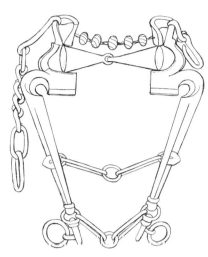

The 'Canon' bit recommended by the sixteenth-century British authority Thomas Blundeville. The beads above the mouthpiece were to encourage salivation

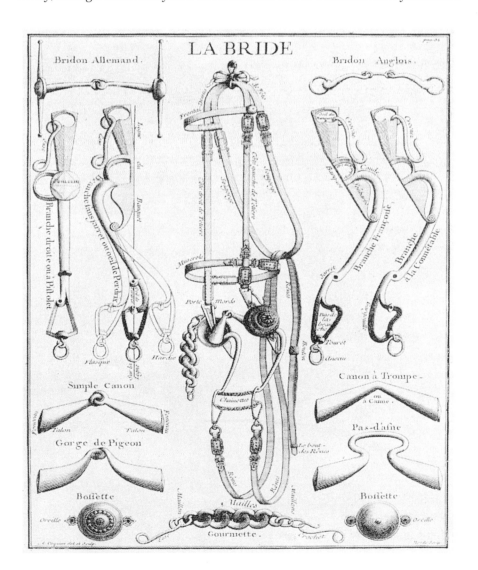

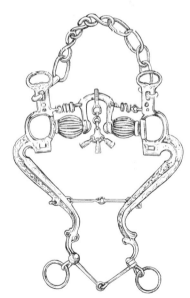

This sixteenth-century bit used by Henry VIII is a strange mix of keys, rollers and swivelled port. One wonders what the horse thought of it. The bit is, however, an early example of the Pelham

Left: A page from the book Ecole de Cavalerie *by the 'Father of Classical Equitation', Francois Robichon de la Guérinière (1688–1751). The book was adopted as 'holy writ' by Vienna's Spanish Riding School*

35

Grisone, when horses were lighter and more responsive, coercion had given way to the concept of riding as the rational science exemplified by Guérinière. The principles he propounded remain, virtually inviolate, at the very heart of twentieth-century classicism as it is preserved at the Spanish School, also at Saumur, and in the classical institutions of Spain and Portugal.

So far as bitting was concerned, the military schools of Europe, themselves founded on classicism, ensured that the accent remained firmly on the curb bit up to and beyond the turn of the nineteenth and twentieth centuries.

NINETEENTH AND TWENTIETH CENTURIES – THE ART AND SCIENCE

The nineteenth century produced a greater variety of bits and bitting combinations than ever before, and the twentieth, up to World War II, was, if anything, even more prolific, embracing with enthusiasm the new legion of ingeniously designed Pelhams, as well as some extraordinarily inventive innovations in other bitting groups.

Modern equestrian thinking is generally derisive about the practice of

A massively ugly German bit of the seventeenth-century, but with a mouthpiece that is not inhumane

the military schools that dominated equestrian Europe – and to a large degree the USA also, up to the turn of the century – and remained a powerful influence for a few years after World War II. But then modern thinking can be dismissive of almost anything outside its immediate experience.

Of course, the standards attained at horse trials, showjumping and dressage are immeasurably higher than ever before, but then the scale of equestrian activity has been similarly expanded. What is not sufficiently appreciated is that many military riders were, by any criteria, exceptional horsemen. Their standards of horse management, certainly between the two wars, far exceeded those generally practised today and their meticulous approach to the details of mouth conformation and bit structure in relation to carriage and movement came near to elevating the science of bitting to an art in its own right.

Even so, and despite the example of Federico Caprilli and his insistence upon the snaffle at the beginning of the twentieth century, they continued for the most part to see the snaffle as the necessary introduction to the curb, and considered that it was the curb which would complete the business

Left: This charming study by Baron Reis d'Eisenberg shows an elegant horseman preserving the classical tradition of contact through the weight of the rein

A lithograph exemplifying the classicism of the Iberian school. The top rein is attached to a probably strengthened, cereta-type noseband in which the horse would have been schooled initially. The collection of the horse in the execution of the piaffe *is perfection*

of making the mouth and encouraging the build-up of muscles which would result in the horse arching the neck, raising the shoulder and becoming light in hand.

Now it is the day of the snaffle, made by cheap Eastern labour that may have no contact with horses at all. Nine riders out of ten would have little idea of how to introduce the curb bit or to teach the necessary preliminary flexions. Indeed, very few riders will ever ride other than in a snaffle in a whole lifetime.

Under the circumstances that may not be a bad idea!

Captain Federico Caprilli (1868–1907) whose forward system of riding with its insistence upon the snaffle represent a landmark in equestrian history, dividing one era of horsemanship from the next

Part II

PRINCIPLES & MECHANICS

PRINCIPLES
AND MECHANICS

The bit has enormous potential to improve balance, outline, freedom and the smoothness of the paces. It contributes substantially, therefore, in producing a horse that is a pleasure to ride; however, it is by no means the panacea for all equestrian ills. Indeed, all too often its use is counter-productive in all those desirable respects, for the reason that the rider is insufficiently competent to use the bit (in effect, the hand) as a part of the combination of interdependent aids, or indeed perhaps to appreciate its role within that combination. Those are major factors in the misuse, and sometimes the abuse, of the bit, though obviously a badly fitting bridle, or a bitting arrangement that is unsuitable for the mouth conformation of the individual horse, will both contribute to an unsatisfactory result that may be made blatantly manifest in the horse's behaviour and outline.

To put the bit into perspective it has to be seen as part of the whole business of riding, never being viewed or *used* in isolation. The simile of the Equitational Wheel, the horseman's equivalent of the Buddhist Wheel of Life, in which all elements are harmonious, is a good starting point to understanding the role of the bit.

The Equitational Wheel comprises a hub and four spokes. The HUB represents the rider's seat – secure, in balance, and independent of the reins, the latter being 'a consummation devoutly to be wished' but infinitely more difficult to achieve in practice. To approach that equestrian Nirvana demands much dedication, application and a lot of painstaking work on the lunge under a good instructor.

The four spokes are the aids, the signals given to the horse. These are made with the parts of the body which make up the physical discipline of riding, and the fourth belongs to the mental discipline, which is just as important. This last is the **head** aid, since thought – even subconscious thought – and for but the merest split second, must precede physical action. When the physical aid is made thoughtlessly it may also be irrational.

The three physical aids are produced by the **legs**; the **trunk** and **body-**

The Equitational Wheel. The spokes in the horseman's equivalent of the Buddhist Wheel of Life represent the riding aids which are the means of communication between horse and rider

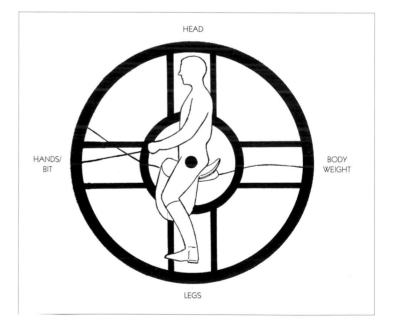

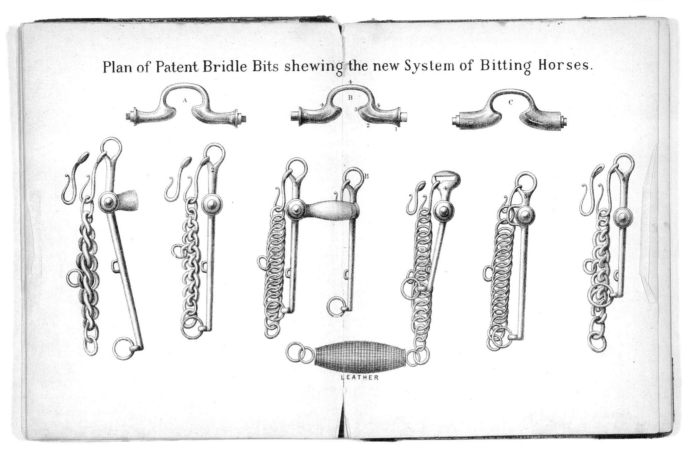

Plan of Patent Bridle Bits shewing the new System of Bitting Horses.

weight, of course, and the **hand** acting through the agency of the bit, which supports and follows the aids given by legs, seat and trunk. The hand should always, by however infinitesimal a period, be the *last link* in the chain of the riding aids.

Should the rider be ineffectual in the application of the legs, whether used in concert or singly, or if the upper body is insufficiently balanced, soft and supple to conform to the movement of the horse, and in some instances to influence it, then the Wheel itself will be affected by the weakness of its component parts. If the **hub**, the rider's seat, is at fault, which it is likely to be if there is malfunctioning of the physical aids, then the Wheel collapses.

It follows incontrovertibly that the bit, whatever the type employed, becomes more or less effective according to the ability of the rider and, of course, the level of the horse's training, since that is bound to be relative to the responses made to the aids.

It is not unreasonable to speculate that money expended by riders searching for 'the key to every horse's mouth' would be better spent on a course of riding lessons. The saying originated with Benjamin Latchford, the London loriner, and appeared in his treatise *The Loriner*, published in 1883. A couple of paragraphs later, Latchford wrote that of every twenty bits he made, nineteen were for men's heads and one for the horse's.

An illustration from Don Juan Segundo's treatise on bitting (1832) which appeared in Benjamin Latchford's The Loriner

The title page from Latchford's famous 'Opinions and Observations'

THE LORINER.

OPINIONS AND OBSERVATIONS ON

BRIDLE-BITS

AND THE

SUITABLE BITTING OF HORSES,

WITH ILLUSTRATIONS

BY

BENJAMIN LATCHFORD,

Bridle-Bit, Stirrup, and Spur Maker

TO

HER MAJESTY, H.R.H. THE PRINCE OF WALES, Etc.

11, UPPER ST. MARTIN'S LANE, LONDON, W.C.

London:
PRINTED BY HERBERT FITCH & CO., LONDON & YARD PRINTING WORKS, 30, BURY STREET, E.C.
1883.

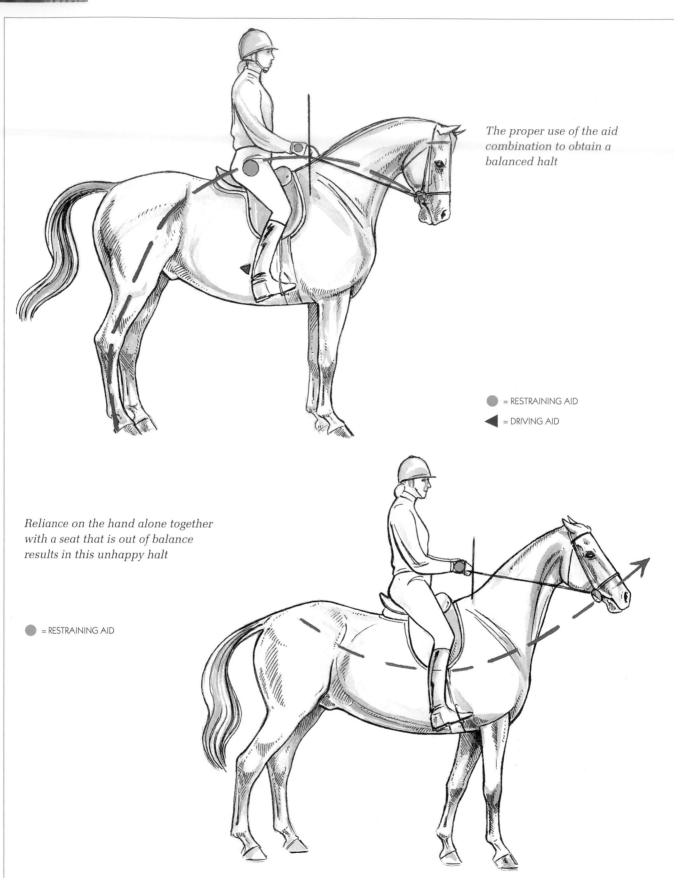

The proper use of the aid combination to obtain a balanced halt

● = RESTRAINING AID

◀ = DRIVING AID

Reliance on the hand alone together with a seat that is out of balance results in this unhappy halt

● = RESTRAINING AID

THE OBJECT

Simplistically, the bit is implicit to control, and when used in conjunction with the remaining aids serves as a sort of combined steering wheel (in part) and brake. In some instances that may be sufficient, but as a definition it is incomplete and so open to extension.

In rational, educated riding a primary role of the bit is to govern the impulsion created by the legs and seat, which causes the hindlegs to be engaged further under the body with maximum flexion of the joints. The energy, or the propulsive thrust that is produced as a result, can either be contained by the hand, in which case the outline will be shortened, or it can be released to a predetermined degree to lower and lengthen the outline. In both instances the horse is required to work within the frame imposed by the legs at one end and the hand at the other.

Furthermore, the direction of the forward thrust from the quarters can be channelled by the action of the bit to move the shoulders, position the quarters or to shift both simultaneously when it is applied in one or other of the five *rein effects*, discussed later in this chapter.

It follows, of course, that the hand and the bit, which are, after all, synonymous, are more or less effective in direct ratio to the impulsion

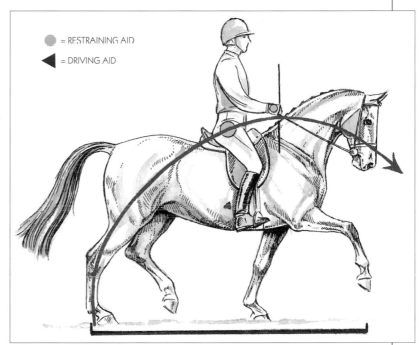

= RESTRAINING AID

= DRIVING AID

Above and left: The aids supplied to obtain collection and a shortening of the outline

created. Without impulsion the horse is like a boat becalmed, when the use of the rudder will produce no result at all. Taking these factors into account, the control imposed by the bit can be defined to flesh out the bare bones of the brake-cum-steering wheel concept:

1 It assists when used in conjunction with the legs and the disposition of the bodyweight to make changes of direction or turns to either hand or when moving laterally, and can control the positioning of the horse through the placement of shoulders and quarters.

2 It regulates the pace and effects the transitions from one to another when applied following the action of the legs. (In alterations made within a pace, or in transitions, leg action precedes that of the hand, if only by a minimal degree. In effect, the horse is pushed into a more direct contact with the bit.)

3 It follows that the bit, the principal restraining aid, can also act, in conjunction with the driving aids, to produce alterations in outline, ie the shortening and lengthening of the horse's base.

NOTE: From the purist viewpoint the bit is

Below and below left: Application of the aids to produce extension

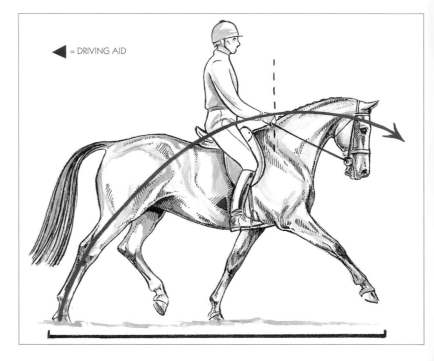

= DRIVING AID

supportive of, and subservient to the driving aids, but in practice there will be occasions when the hand is applied in a more dominant, restraining role and it would be foolish, and even pie-in-the-sky, to pretend otherwise.

A big, strong, very fit, bold horse galloping over a cross-country course, studded with formidable obstacles designed to test the courage and physical ability of both horse and rider at the ultimate level, will on occasions need to be restrained decisively if the combination is not to come to grief. The rider's leg will almost certainly remain in passive, steady contact, the trunk will be straightened and the shoulder brought back, but the hand may act strongly to give a short, sharp check and increase the rider's control over the approach. It is a question of re-imposing balance – *both physically and mentally.*

Similarly, the half-halt employed to maintain or correct the balance within the school will be employed more strongly to correct the approach in a jumping competition. The effect of the legs driving the horse onto a somewhat raised, momentarily resistant hand shortens the outline, places the weight more over the quarters and lightens the forehand to put the horse into an increased state of balance.

DIRECTIONAL CHANGES AND REIN EFFECTS

Possibly the most widely held misconception is that which maintains that the position of the head, as dictated by the bit, governs the directional movement; but since head and neck move independently of the rest of the

Below: Maintenance or correction of the balance by the half-halt made by the judicious use of restraining and driving aids

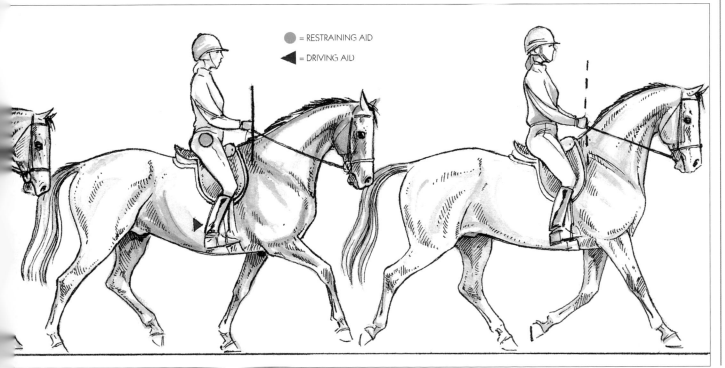

= RESTRAINING AID

= DRIVING AID

body, it patently does not do this. The directional movement is in fact governed by the quarters, which are connected to the shoulders, and where the quarters point there the horse must go.

Changes of direction are made by positioning the quarters and are then executed with the head leading the movement in response to the indications made by the bit. It is quite possible for the head to point to the left while the horse moves to the right. In fact, if the head is pulled round to the left it actually makes it easier for the horse to move to the right, the reason being that the left shoulder is to all intents closed and so prohibits movement in that direction, whilst the right shoulder is correspondingly opened. (Watch a small child on a determined, worldly-wise pony that is intent upon turning right-handed in opposition to his rider's wishes. The child will pull his head round with the left rein so that his muzzle touches his girth, but it will not prevent the pony going in the opposite direction.)

REIN EFFECTS

It is probable that the majority of riders know very little, if anything at all, about the five rein effects, which when correctly applied can transform the bit into an instrument of great precision. They are rarely included in riding instruction as a composite entity, although they are generally recognised in academic equitation. But they are practised, sometimes almost unconsciously, by most serious riders.

In fact, it is easy enough to understand the rein effects, although more difficult to put them into practice effectively, and it would be disastrous for any one rein to be used in isolation. Each rein must be supported at all times by its partner, and of course there has to be sustained impulsion supporting the action of both. In perfection all five are moulded into one harmonious whole, and that requires some degree of sensitivity in the use of the hand, as well as the ability to create impulsion.

Without doubt, mastery of the rein (bit) effects increases the rider's ability to position the horse with some finesse. They are also necessary to counteract deviations and evasions that can arise in the shoulders and quarters, and so they assist very materially in 'straightening' the horse – that is, in encouraging the hind feet to follow directly in the track of the fore feet without being carried out to one side or the other.

Perhaps as much as anything a knowledge of the rein (bit) effects helps us in recognising incorrect uses of the bit or, indeed, those which are in contradiction to the movement required.

The five effects comprise two *direct* and three *indirect* reins, three of the five being reins of *opposition*.

A *direct* rein acts on the same side as it is applied. *Indirect* reins act conversely, on the opposite side to that on which they are applied.

A rein of *opposition* blocks or opposes the forward thrust provided by

46

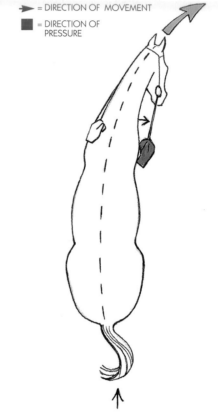

➤ = DIRECTION OF MOVEMENT

■ = DIRECTION OF PRESSURE

Direct rein

the quarters on the side on which it is applied. By doing so it re-channels the thrust of the movement either through the shoulders or the quarters or, in the last of the rein effects, through both to move the whole horse laterally.

THE FIVE REINS

1 **Direct or opening rein** used on turns and circles when the horse is bent to the inside with head and neck aligned to the direction of the movement. It is the easiest aid for the horse to understand and is retained in less exaggerated form in advanced work.

In the turn to the right, for instance, the right rein is carried slightly outwards whilst the left rein supports its partner by being 'given' to allow the bend, an action that must occur if the rider looks in the direction of the turn when the left shoulder will be carried a little in advance of the right. In fact, given that the rein contact is equal the turn is made by the ceding of the *outside* rein (the left, in this instance) and so the rider, employing the right leg actively to encourage the further engagement of the horse's inside hind, is riding 'from the inside leg into the outside hand'.

= DIRECTION OF MOVEMENT

= DIRECTION OF PRESSURE

Indirect rein

2 **Indirect rein.** This is the neck-rein which has been with us since the beginning of equestrian history. It can be used with either or both hands and is, of course, integral to the training of the polo pony.

There is a certain shift of the bit across the mouth and some pressure exerted on its outer edge on the side opposite the direction of the movement. The primary action, however, is that of the rein against the neck.

Applied on the left of the neck it causes head and neck to be bent in that direction but compels the movement of the right shoulder forward and to the right and vice-versa.

It is used in turns and elements of circles calling for an *outside* bend, as in the case of a turn on the forehand, for instance. The rein can also be used in an effective corrective capacity to straighten the horse.

3 **Direct rein of opposition.** This third effect blocks the surge of movement on the side on which it is applied. If, for instance, the right rein is used, the thrust from the quarters, generated by the legs, is opposed by the bit acting on the *right* side of the mouth. In consequence, whilst the head will be carried a little to the *right*, the quarters are shifted to the *left*. This effect can be used in the forehand turn, and, with both reins, in the rein-back where sustained movement forward is reversed. NOTE: It is probable that this is the most misunderstood and misused hand aid in the equestrian compendium.

Quite illogically, this rein of opposition is all too frequently used in

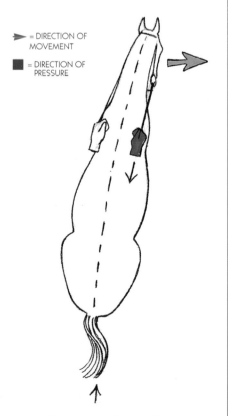

= DIRECTION OF MOVEMENT

= DIRECTION OF PRESSURE

Direct rein of opposition

47

making turns and riding circles when it causes hand and leg to be at cross purposes, disturbs the rhythm, shortens the stride and impedes forward movement. When the inside hand is applied in this way the quarters swing outwards and the rider, in an effort to prevent that undesirable shift from the track, has to act behind the girth with the outside leg, and is often instructed to do just that. The outward swing has, in fact, been caused by the application of the inside rein and it must surely be irrational in the extreme to create a problem with one action and seek to correct it with another.

4 **Indirect rein of opposition in front of the withers.** This is the rein that controls the shoulders, moving them left or right according to which rein is applied. It also causes a secondary movement of the quarters in the opposite direction. Of course, it can be used to make a turn on the centre with outside bend, but its great value is as a corrective rein to hold or shift the shoulder as required.

5 **Indirect rein of opposition behind the withers.** It is the most powerful of the rein effects and is often termed intermediary, and sometimes eulogised as the 'Queen of Reins'.

   Directed towards the horse's opposite hip (without ever *crossing* the wither – the most heinous of equestrian crimes) it moves the whole horse sideways and forwards by acting on both shoulders and quarters. It is used in leg-yielding exercises and in the shoulder-in movement.

■ = DIRECTION OF PRESSURE

Indirect rein of opposition front of the withers

Right and far right: Leg-yielding and shoulder-in demonstrating use of indirect rein of opposition behind the withers

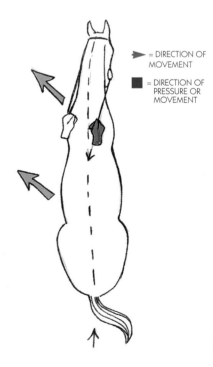

➤ = DIRECTION OF MOVEMENT

■ = DIRECTION OF PRESSURE OR MOVEMENT

Indirect rein of opposition behind the withers

Part III

BITS AND BITTING

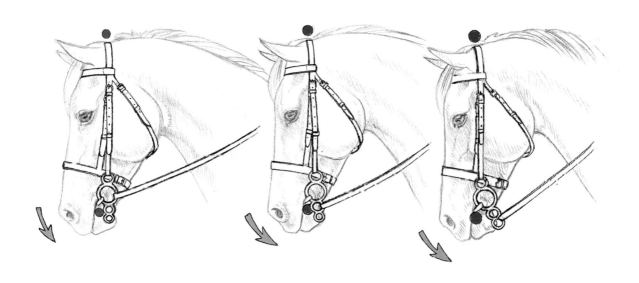

BASIC PRINCIPLES

Despite some modern variations in bit patterns, the principles of bitting can be summarised as involving five groups of bits acting on one or more of seven parts of the horse's head.

There has been one new concept in the history of the bit since the invention of the curb bit by the Celts, but for the moment the Wellep bit, following a construction problem is not available.

Should the bit re-appear it would not be too much to claim that it represents 'a new concept in bitting'. The principal feature of this nearly perfectly engineered piece of equipment is the cable passing through the jointed mouthpiece to which the reins are attached at either end. It allows, as it were, a continuous loop between the rider's hands, allowing him to feel with one hand the action of the other. If the 'lever' cheek piece is used some pressure is applied to the poll to encourage flexion in that part of the head. The control that can be exerted by the Wellep is considerable but the bit nontheless provides a very high degree of comfort and is unlikely to provoke resistance.)

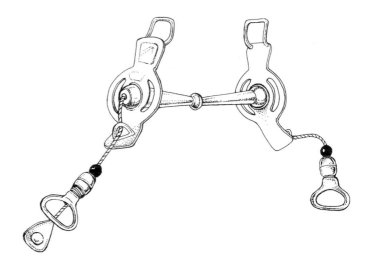

The Wellep bit that might have altered much of the theory of bitting and provided a new concept in equitation

The five bit groups are:
1 Snaffle
2 Weymouth/Ward Union double bridle
3 Pelham
4 Gag
5 Nose bridle, known also as the bitless bridle or, less correctly, as the hackamore.

All five act on one or more of seven parts of the horse's head:
1 Corners of the lips
2 Bars
3 Tongue and (to a degree) tongue channel
4 Curb groove
5 Poll
6 Roof of the mouth (rare)
7 Nose, when a bitless bridle is used or when some particular auxiliary is employed. Indeed, the action can be strengthened or be altered in its complexion by the addition of auxiliaries such as martingales and
nosebands.

THE LAW OF THE BIT

From that there follows what may be termed as the Law of the Bit and it is this: the action and pressures applied through the agency of the bit to the head and mouth vary in intensity and character according to four factors:

1 The construction of the bit
2 The conformation of the mouth
3 The angle at which the mouth is carried in relation to the hand
4 The type and fitting of any accessory to the principal bit action

The action of the bit and the subsequent result become more or less effective in relation to the rider's ability to use the supporting aids. It follows that in order to understand the subject and to realise the full potential of the bit it is necessary to have knowledge of:

1 The types of bit available, the variations in design occurring within a bit group, and the resultant action of each
2 The parts of the head and mouth involved in fitting a bridle, and the consequence of pressures being applied to them
3 The effect of auxiliaries on the bit's action, and the types available
4 The conformation of the mouth

These requirements are covered in the following chapters on the bit groups and accessories, and in the chapter "The Mouth and Fitting".

The seven parts of the head that are involved in the principles of bitting

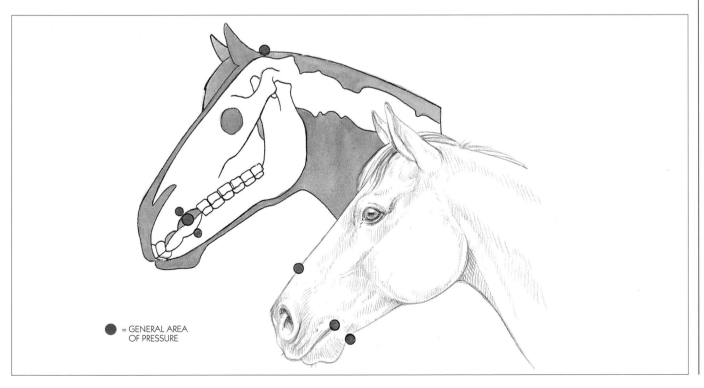

● = GENERAL AREA OF PRESSURE

THE SNAFFLE

This is the largest of the bitting groups, and in our present riding context, arguably the most important. There are numerous sub-divisions within the group and an increasing number of variations on the basic theme introduced by market-conscious manufacturers, who may sometimes add to the confusion by some gross inaccuracies in the naming of their products.

In many instances, perhaps most, the snaffle today is used in conjunction with one or other of the auxiliary nosebands designed to close the mouth and to introduce an additional restraint by acting on the nose. The character of the bit is then altered somewhat and its effect is certainly strengthened.

ACTION

For as long as horsemen have thought rationally about bitting, it has been generally accepted that the snaffle employs a lifting action, upwards against the corners of the lips. In the days when primary emphasis was given to producing flexions at the poll and mouth through the curb bit, the role of the snaffle was to raise the head, neck and shoulders as a prelude to providing a suitable base for the curb to carry out its work.

To a large extent the primary upward action of the snaffle remains unchanged today, but modern riding is infinitely more reliant on the snaffle in the stages of schooling up to advanced level, hence the support of the nosebands. (The straightforward drop noseband has been about since the days of Horenhab and was, indeed, regarded as an integral part of the snaffle bridle in the early cavalry schools of Europe; however, it was not so considered in Britain and Ireland, or indeed in America which, disregarding the tradition of the Western seat, was influenced to a degree by the British practice.)

Below and right: Snaffle bridle

Right: The action of the snaffle corresponding to the relevant head position

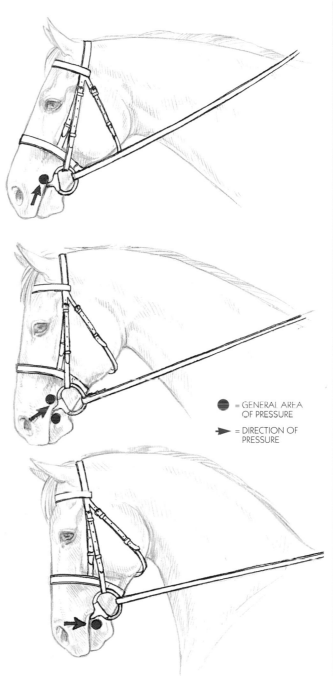

● = GENERAL AREA OF PRESSURE

➤ = DIRECTION OF PRESSURE

Essentially, the action of the snaffle is governed by the position of the head and the relationship of the hand to the horse's mouth. Thus in the early stages of training, when the young horse is encouraged to move 'long and low', the snaffle certainly acts in a largely upwards fashion on the corners of the mouth.

As the training progresses, along with physical development, the horse approaches more of a working

53

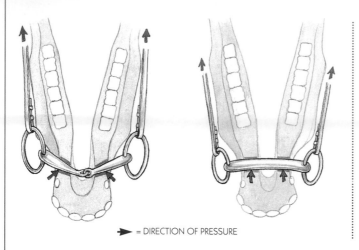

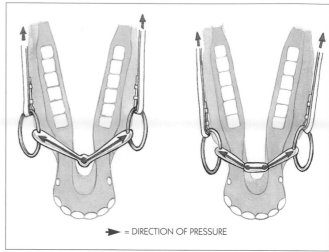

➤ = DIRECTION OF PRESSURE

➤ = DIRECTION OF PRESSURE

Action of snaffle across the lower jaw

Nutcracker action of snaffle and French-link bits

outline. The head carriage is then higher and the face is carried nearer to the vertical plane. In that position the bit acts less upon the corners of the mouth and more across the lower jaw, encouraging a degree of flexion in the latter and a retraction of the nose.

In the more advanced outline when the head is carried on, or close to, the vertical the action is increasingly across the lower jaw.

In both the latter instances, however, there can be a slight upward movement against the corners of the mouth which can, of course, be accentuated by

the sympathetic use of the hand if it becomes necessary to correct the outline, or the contact, by raising the head.

When the bit is 'across the lower jaw' the bearing, in the instance of a jointed mouthpiece, is on the sides of the tongue and possibly upon a part of the bars; by how much depends upon the size and shape of the tongue. Usually, the tongue overlaps the bars by a little, protecting them from direct pressure. A mullen mouthpiece bears more upon the tongue than otherwise.

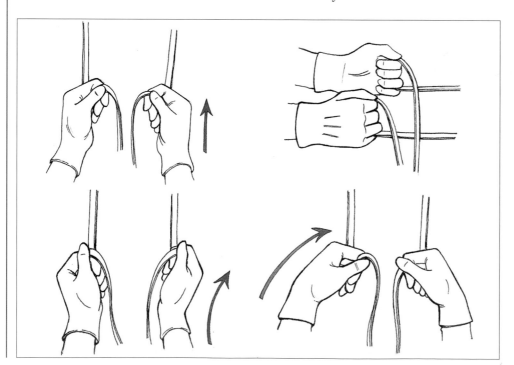

Top: Correct way to hold the snaffle rein

Below: Incorrect but all too frequently seen

➤ = DIRECTION OF MOVEMENT

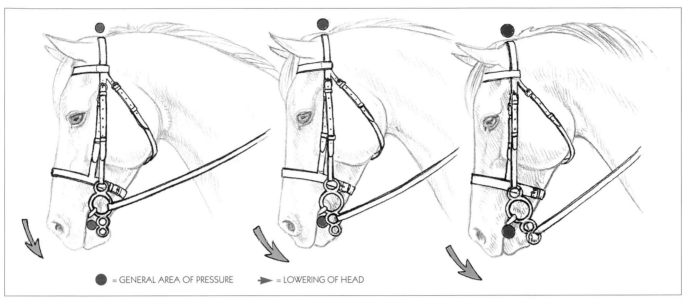

● = GENERAL AREA OF PRESSURE   ➤ = LOWERING OF HEAD

DIVISIONS

Above: Three-ring snaffle. Showing different effects with three different rein positions

The most obvious division in the group is between the **jointed mouthpiece**, with either a single central joint or with a spatula or link joining the two sides of the mouthpiece, and the **straight-bar** or **mullen** (half-moon) mouthpiece. Further divisions occur in the cheeks or bit rings employed.

Of the three, the shaped mullen mouthpiece is the mildest in its effect, particularly when it is thick and made from India rubber or even vulcanite, and even more so when constructed from soft, flexible plastic materials.

The straight metal bar is far more salutary in its

action and can act strongly on the edges of the tongue and the underlying bars. There is a similar tendency with the conventional jointed snaffle but the action is much mitigated by a thick, 'fat' mouthpiece, and, of course, the mouthpiece by its construction allows room for the tongue rather like the port of the curb bit, if in a less sophisticated fashion.

Similarly, a central link or spatula, lying on the tongue, reduces the so-called 'nutcracker' action commensurately as well as lessening the direct pressure on the outside of the bars.

A comparatively recent German innovation is a control/correction snaffle with either loose or eggbutt rings to a **ported mouth**. The port is wide and relatively shallow. It sits comfortably over the tongue with an even pressure being applied to the lower

Jointed mouthpiece

Mullen mouthpiece

Ported mouthpiece

jaw over the bars and it obviates entirely, one would think, any possibility of the tongue being held over the bit.

The only other ported mouth snaffle of significance is the **Fillis* bradoon** which has a very different character. It is *suspended* in the mouth rather than resting on it, and is hinged on either side of the port. It has proved very successful on horses that seem less than comfortable in a plain snaffle because of their tongues. The problem is usually because the

Bar mouth with players

Fillis bradoon. The bit is hinged on either side of the port and is suspended in the mouth

Mouthing bit with players

tongue groove is too shallow to accommodate the tongue comfortably.

Mouthing or **breaking** bits are still made, conventionally, as a straight bar but with the addition of 'keys' set in the centre of the mouthpiece. However, jointed mouthing bits with keys set on a central ring are also available. The purpose of the 'keys' is to keep the mouth wet, ie salivating as the result of the horse playing, or 'mouthing', the bit. The result of a wet, 'soapy' mouth is relaxation in the lower jaw, a prime requirement in training. Conversely, a 'dry' mouth encourages a fixed jaw and is correspondingly unresponsive. A suitable riposte to Benjamin Latchford's assertation that, 'There is a key to every horse's mouth' (*The Loriner*, 1883) might be, 'salivation is the key to every horse's mouth'.

Modern trainers tend not to use breaking bits of this sort nearly so much as in previous years, preferring to

rely on an India rubber mullen mouth snaffle, or the moulded plastics which are soft enough for the mouthpiece to shape itself to the jaw. The thinking behind the preference is that the horse's continual mouthing of a key bit may, and can, become habitual and result in an unsteady head carriage.

Where the conventional key bit is used, great care must be taken in its fitting. All too often it is overlarge, and as if to compound the crime, it is also often fitted too low in the mouth. The trainer is then giving positive encouragement to evasions, including that of getting the tongue over the bit.

Youngstock are often led in a Tattersall's ring bit which is also fitted with keys that are, in truth, more or less irrelevant to the purpose. It is, nonetheless, a pretty powerful form of restraint, on a par with the even sharper Chifney lead bit, referred to by its inventor, the ineffably conceited jockey Samuel Chifney (1753–1807), as an anti-rear bit. If one wished to *encourage* rearing, then this is the bit for the job.

Today the greatest impact on bit design and construction is probably that of the German industry. It

---

*(James Fillis (1834-1913), who was the apostle of *la grande impulsion* and deserves to be numbered among the latter-day masters. Born in London, most of his work was done in Paris, whilst for 10 years he served as Colonel and *Ecuyer-en-chef* at the Czar's Cavalry School at St Petersburg).

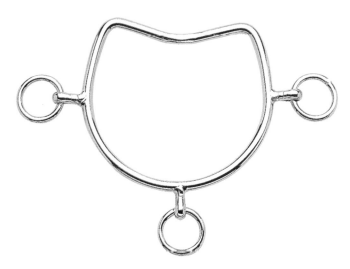

The Chifney 'anti-rear' bit for leading in-hand. An invention of the jockey Samuel Chifney (1753–1807)

A straight mouth variation of the Chifney

CHEEKS

Cheeks, which in this context may be taken to include rings, vary almost as much as mouthpieces and they influence the action similarly. At one end of the spectrum there is the **loose ring** passing through holes in the butt-end of the mouthpiece; at the other the **full cheek**, exemplified by the Fulmer-type snaffles.

The loose ring has the advantage, if one should belong to that school of thought, of allowing movement of the mouthpiece so as to encourage salivation. If fitted snugly, the ring by being pressed against the cheek in response to the action of the opposite rein, will assist the lateral movement of the head. The larger the ring the greater, obviously, will be its influence in this respect, and, moreover, it will counter any evasion of the bit's central action by preventing it being slid through the mouth. If there is a disadvantage it is that the loose ring may pinch the

Tattersall's ring bit. This bit is used to lead youngstock in hand

produces bits of very high quality, with interesting designs that in some instances combine certain of the characteristics of the principal groups – and that may be the way forward. There is, for instance, the 'control' or schooling bit, already mentioned on p.**55,** a snaffle with either a loose or eggbutt ring that has a wide, ported mouthpiece, which makes a lot of bitting sense. (There are also one or two others that fail lamentably to seduce the critical faculty.)

Loose-ring snaffle

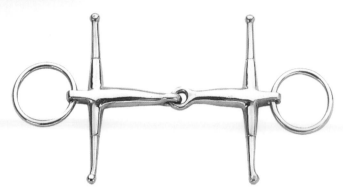

The Fulmer or Australian loose-ring cheek snaffle

lips as the hole through which it passes becomes worn. Regular inspection of the bit should preclude that possibility, however, and pre-empt any natural resistance arising as a result.

Pinching of the lips is obviated by the use of the **eggbutt** cheek, but the design ensures that the bit remains fixed in the mouth and allows no up-and-

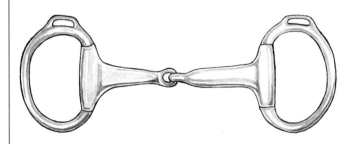

Eggbutt slotted cheek snaffle. This design had the advantage of fixing the bit centrally in the mouth and ensured precise, direct action across the lower jaw

down movement. Whether or not this is an advantage or otherwise depends upon one's viewpoint and, of course, the propensity of the horse to salivate or not to do so. (The best and most logical form of eggbutt cheek was one with a slot cut in the ring to take the cheekpiece of the bridle. It centralised the bit absolutely and directed the action precisely over the lower jaw. Alas, it seems to be in production no longer.)

The eggbutt derived from the **dee cheek** racing snaffle, and dee cheeks are still in general use. In

turn, the dee cheek was a cut-down version of the **full cheek**, which was discarded because it was thought possible that in the event of an accident the cheek might enter into a nostril.

Fixed, full-cheek snaffles remain very much in production alongside the **Fulmer** or **Australian loose-ring, cheek snaffle**. The latter's loose ring allows for some movement in the mouth, although that is largely prevented by the retaining straps fitted from the bridle to the end of the cheeks. The purpose of the

The dee-cheek preceded the Eggbutt design and was a cut-down version of the full cheek snaffle

retainers, other than to act as a safeguard against the cheek ends getting caught up in a nostril, is to maintain the bit's position in the mouth, which they do very effectively.

The prime purpose of cheeks on the snaffle is to prevent the bit sliding through the mouth and they also assist the lateral action by pressing up against the animal's face.

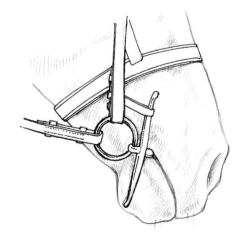

Retaining straps secured to the cheek of a Fulmer snaffle

Right: A bit of German design termed a 'correction' bit. The mouthpiece is curved back at each side and the ported mouth gives a very positive contact to the bars

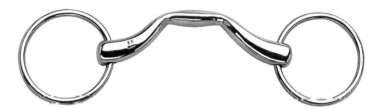

Left: A very useful ported snaffle of German manufacture. It ensures freedom for the tongue

Right: A loose ring snaffle with a carefully shaped mouthpiece of moderate weight: a German product

Left: The rounded mouthpiece of this loose-ring snaffle is possibly softer than that of the bit above

Right: A German-made eggbutt snaffle with a rounded central spatula

Left: A Dr Bristol with eggbutt cheeks. There is a possibility of the edge of the spatula bearing upon the tongue, which is obviously neither comfortable nor desirable

Left: Somewhat grandiloquently, this is called a 'training' bit. In fact it is no more than a tarted-up French bradoon, but none the worse for that

Right: This excellent snaffle has a copper spatula. Whether that is an advantage or not is arguable

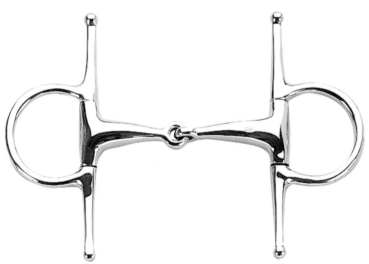

Left: A particularly well-made full cheek snaffle with a superbly-shaped mouthpiece

Right: This one has a copper roller at its centre. It reduced the 'nutcracker' effect but is really no more than a fashionable conceit

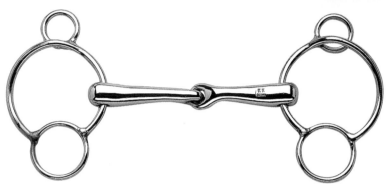

Right: This is called a 'Universal' bit, which it is not. However, it is a useful example of a 'two-ringed' snaffle and the independent eye is an interesting feature

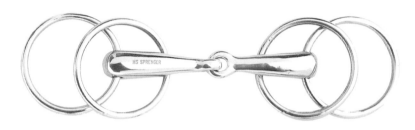

Left: Our old friend the Wilson four-ring snaffle in ultra-modern form

Right: A very mild bit, a rubber mullen mouth snaffle

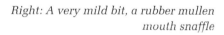

Left: In the interests of reduced weight this snaffle has a hollow mouthpiece

Right: A resilient, polyurethane snaffle with a mouth allowing room for the tongue

Left: A soft, jointed snaffle covered in rubber

Right: A rubber snaffle with a lightweight mouthpiece that would be suitable for a very sensitive mouth

Left: A race-weight snaffle

Right: A lightweight shallow ported snaffle

Left: Mullen mouth of either rubber or vulcanite fitted with dee-cheeks which, in part, will prevent it being pulled through the mouth

Right: Straightforward eggbutt snaffle with mouthpiece of moderate weight

Right: Straight bar bit of the kind used for showing stallions. It has a serrated mouthpiece for greater effect

Left: The classic French bradoon that reduced the 'nutcracker' effect and rests comfortably on the tongue

Right: A Waterford link snaffle with copper rollers, which horses are supposed to appreciate

Left: Dick Christian's snaffle with central ring on the same principle as the dividing spatula. (Dick Christian was a hard-riding, Leicestershire thruster of the nineteenth century)

Right: A chain snaffle, which is not nearly so severe as it seems

Left: Jointed polyurethane mouth, eggbutt snaffle

Right: The same as above with loose rings

Left: A more interestingly shaped mouth of polyurethane which horses seem to appreciate, if for no good reason

Right: A variation on the wavy mouthpiece which is a feature of the 'Happy Mouth' bits, some of which are apple flavoured!

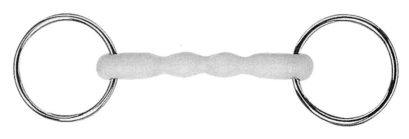

Left: Baucher's snaffle named after François Baucher, the controversial nineteenth-century French genius who displayed his art in the Parisian theatres. Like the Fillis bradoon the bit is 'suspended' in the mouth

Right: This might be called a tongue snaffle designed to keep the tongue in place under the mouthpiece

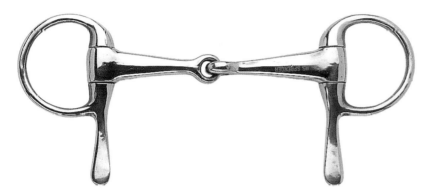

Left: Half-spoon cheek eggbutt snaffle used as a trotting bit

Right: The Dexter ring bit – shades of the North African Mameluke bit. It is a recognised 'stopper', the ring forming a second mouthpiece, and is much used in trotting

Left: This is called a 'hollow Mouth Salivation' snaffle and is the most ridiculous bit in the book

MULTI-RINGS

Other than those obvious sub-divisions in the group there are latter-day arrivals fitted with 'multi-ring' cheeks. They almost overlap into the Pelham and curb groups, but not quite since they employ no curb chain. What is confusing is that some patterns are described variously as 'elevators' or either American or Dutch 'gags'.

By definition a 'gag' operates with an accentuated snaffle action to raise the head, but that is certainly not the action of these curiously mis-named bits – just the opposite in fact. Central to the action of the snaffle is the absence of curb action dependent upon the system of levers, and so to call a conventional Pelham – curb chain and all – an 'Argentine snaffle', for instance, is arrant nonsense and an example of disturbing ignorance to boot. But then we have the American 'long shank' snaffle, which has a cheek 6–7in (15–18cm) long and which is no more than a curb bit minus the customary curb chain.

Nevertheless, if only because it is with us in some numbers, the multi-ring, usually two or three rings, fitted to a single mouthpiece is legitimate enough and not an unattractive concept – perhaps, indeed, it should be regarded as the sixth bitting group. The idea is to have a multi-purpose bit whose action varies according to the position of the rein. Use the rein on the top ring and you have ordinary snaffle action – well, nearly: in fact since the small ring to which the bridle cheeks are attached is set above the top rein there will also be some nominal downward pressure on the poll, which has the effect of *lowering* the head.

Place the rein on the lower ring, and the poll pressure is increased as well as the pressure across the lower jaw – and that, despite the absence of a curb chain, is very close to the action of a curb bit. It is possible, of course, to use two reins on the bit, one on top and one below *à la* Pelham, in fact. One notable German manufacturer describes the effect as being that of 'a weakened Weymouth', and then spoils it all by stating that a single rein used on the lower ring has 'the effect of a weakened Weymouth combined with that of a *gag* bit'. One can only say that the quality of his product exceeds his knowledge of the science of bitting.

It is also suggested that a multi-ring bit can be used with Pelham roundings (a strap that joins the top and bottom rings and to which the rein is attached; however, the degree of finesse then obtainable reduces the bit to little more than a blunt instrument.

Obviously there is a place for the multi-ring snaffle, although for the present it is unlikely to be acceptable bitting for dressage tests. Like everything, there are disadvantages, and in this instance the construction is not ideal to the hand opening, as in the first direct-rein effect, to ride circles or elements of circles.

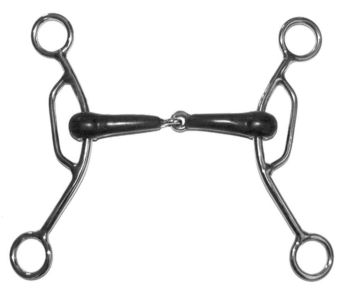

This is the quaintly named American Gag, sometimes termed an 'elevator' bit. It may be American but it is not a gag and whilst it will lower the head by poll pressure it will never act to raise it

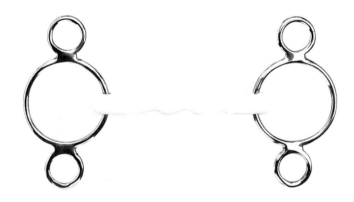

Again, this is termed a 'gag' which it is patently not. It is, in fact, an example of a two-ring snaffle with the possibility of lowering action, fitted to a well-shaped polyurethane mouthpiece.

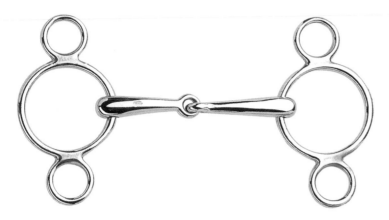

Left: Another two-ring snaffle with the ability to lower the head when the rein is fitted to the lower ring

Right: Three rings this time with an increased potential for lowering the head by poll pressure

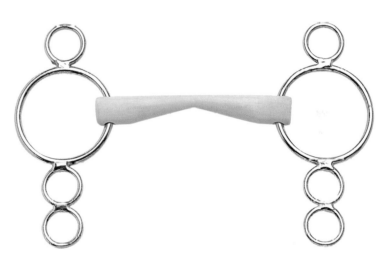

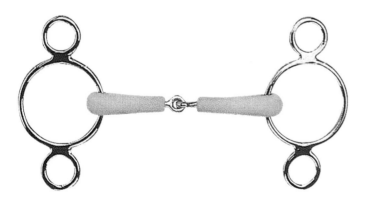

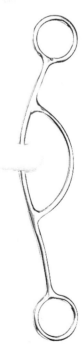

Above: Same ring cheek with soft, polyurethane mouthpiece

Right: The misnamed 'elevator' – really a curb bit without the curb chain. This one has the sensible polyurethane mouthpiece

STRONG SNAFFLES

One section of the snaffle grouping can rightly be termed as 'strong' in their effect. Obvious 'stoppers' are the snaffles with **twisted** mouthpieces which can be very severe if they are of small diameter. A mouthpiece made of twisted wire, whether it be made of copper or even gold, is barbaric and has no place in educated riding.

Rollers, placed either round the bit (as in classical Greece) or set across the mouthpiece, are a different matter. Such bits are far less severe than might be imagined and are distinctly useful on a strong, ongoing horse who has his heart in the right place but may be a bit exuberant. Rollers prevent the horse taking hold of the bit (taking 'the bit between his teeth'), and the movement seems to encourage relaxation in the lower jaw.

The **Magenis** (originally 'MacGuiness') has rollers set across the mouth, and is a deterrent to the animal which attempts to evade the bit by crossing his jaw. Used in a soft, gliding movement across the mouth by the fingers of each hand acting alternately, it will bring down the head and produce flexion at the poll and in the lower jaw.

Deserving of the term 'stopper' is the **Scorrier** or **Cornish snaffle** with its serrated mouthpiece and four rings. It produces a very strong, direct, squeezing effect on the mouth through the inside rings attached to the bridle cheeks, and allows the rein to act with considerable force.

Even less sensible is the **Y-** or **W-mouth** with its two thin mouthpieces, their joints set one on either side. It can cause pinching and bruising of the lips and tongue and is not a pleasant bit. Nor, of course, and for much the same reasons, are the *spring* or *butterfly clips*

Left: Twisted double-wire snaffle. It has no place in humane or educated riding

Right: A twisted snaffle mouthpiece which is severe and in most instances unnecessary

Left: Rollers round the mouth. They encourage relaxation in the lower jaw and whilst potentially strong are not severe

Left: A neat copper roller snaffle that is a popular and effective competition bit

Right: The Magenis snaffle features rollers set across the mouth. The arrangement effectively deters attempts to cross the jaws

Left: The Scorrier or Cornish snaffle with its serrated mouthpiece and squeezing action is essentially a strong, 'stopping' bit

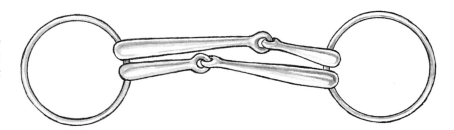

Right: The Y or W mouth bit can cause pinching and bruising and is not a pleasant piece of equipment

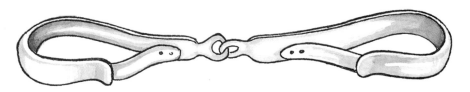

Left: The Butterfly clip is yet another stopping device. Thankfully, it is not much seen today

SPECIALIST BRIDLES

The three bridles known as the Newmarket, Rockwell and Norton, are representative of a group based on the four-ring **Wilson snaffle**, which is also used as a simple driving bit. The majority of bridles of this type are confined to harness racing but the three selected are riding bridles.

The simplest and probably the most practical of the three is the **Newmarket** training bridle, which despite its name is unlikely to be seen at the headquarters of racing. It originated at the British cavalry school at Weedon, where it acquired the name Newmarket, and it may have been an improvement on a previous pattern.

The bit used is a four-ring mullen-mouth snaffle, the headpiece and a noseband being fitted to the inside rings. The outside rings carry the reins. Used with either one or two reins its purpose was to lower

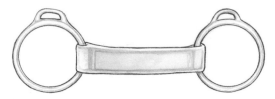

The Weedon Flat-mouth snaffle. It covered a large area of sensory nerves and was used very successfully in the days when Weedon was the British cavalry school

the nose and it was seen as a sensible introduction to the double bridle. Brigadier Bowden-Smith, an Olympic rider between the Wars and at one time an instructor at Weedon, described it thus:

It is an excellent form of snaffle for training a young horse for it can be adjusted to take a considerable amount of pressure on the nose, thus saving the sensitive young mouth. By using the rein on the top or noseband ring only, the mouth can be completely rested.

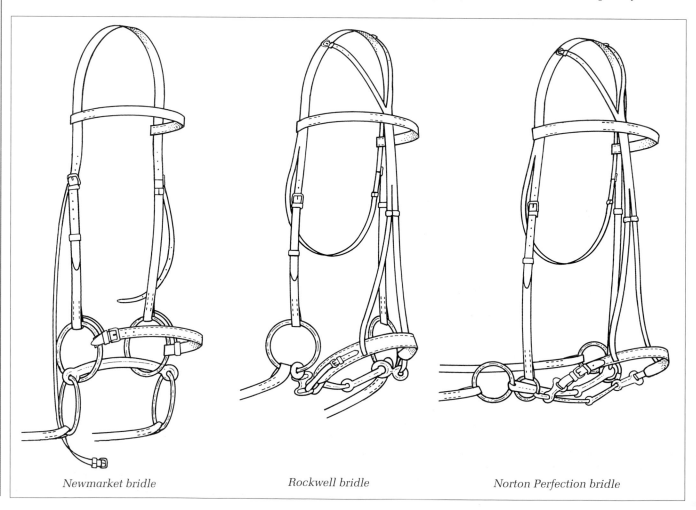

Newmarket bridle   Rockwell bridle   Norton Perfection bridle

The bridle is vastly superior to any combination of cavesson and snaffle*, with one pair of reins attached to the rings of the cavesson and one pair to the snaffle. This is a cumbersome contrivance and makes horses' noses and lips sore.

The **Rockwell** and the **Norton Perfection** (also called the **Citation** after a famous racehorse who benefited from its firm restraint) belong to the sport of racing (although either could form an effective braking system for a hard-pulling horse competing in cross-country events). The carefully constructed Rockwell is the milder of the two, employing a thickish snaffle

A Norton Perfection bridle worn by a harness racer

Below: Detail of the Norton bit

fitted with figure-of-eight links in place of the Newmarket's inside pair of rings. To these loops are attached an adjustable elastic noseband supported by a bifurcated face strap which can be adjusted to raise the bit in the mouth.

Control is imposed by a combination of nose and bit pressure, and of course there is the powerful

---

*(The reference is to the practice dating from the Renaissance schools, which was, at that time, still carried on in the influential German cavalry schools and, indeed, at the Spanish Riding School in Vienna, British cavalry officer of the period may have had their faults but they were for the most part gifted and humane and consummate horsemasters. What is more they could express themselves in plain, lucid English!).

71

psychological restraint of the face strap. This is a suitable bridle for a strong horse, without itself being strong or severe in its action.

The Norton is less subtle and might be considered to have the potential to stop a runaway train. There are four rings to the bridle and two mouthpieces, the secondary one being of the thin wire type. It is to the latter that the noseband is attached by means of the metal loops fitted to the mouthpiece. It is a powerful enough piece of equipment to bring to mind the old horseman's adage, 'you can always stop a horse but can you make him go again?'.

DIAMETER

Finally there is the matter of the bit's diameter, which is critical to the horse's performance, in general a broad, thick mouthpiece being kinder and more effective than a narrow, pencil-thin one.

A broad mouthpiece bears upon a correspondingly broad surface and, in consequence, on a greater number of sensory nerves, the nerves of feeling that are very close to the surface in the mouth, the lips and tongue. These nerves lead to the brain, culminating in the centres of memory and consciousness.

Conversely, the sharp, narrow mouthpiece concentrates the pressure over a very small area, with the result that the nerves are soon numb and deadened to sensation. The mouth then becomes insensitive, and may even be calloused by the continual pressure. In those circumstances the horse's mouth will be hardened and he is likely to become a strong puller. At that point there is often a temptation to add to the braking equipment, fitting more and more extraneous restraints – and that is a sure way of ensuring that matters go from bad to worse.

Providing one's nerve is up to it, it will be far more satisfactory to fit the softest, thickest bit available, on the sure principle that horses pull *against* pain, and become more responsive when the source of discomfort is removed.

It is worth remembering, besides being fundamental to the art of bitting, that it is the uninterrupted dead pull of the hand that provokes a comparable reaction from the horse. The only way to hold a pulling horse is for the hand to act intermittently, the fingers *taking* (pretty decisively) as the horse 'takes' and giving when he gives. To add to the strength of the message it is often effective if one hand is fixed on the wither whilst the other is raised a little and acts in an unmistakeably decisive manner.

Otherwise, commend your soul to your Maker, push your hat down and pretend you want to go that fast.

The British Team rider, Ginny Leng, jumping confidently with the horse in a Rockwell bridle

THE DOUBLE BRIDLE

Although the emphasis in modern riding is fixed firmly on the snaffle, the double bridle retains its importance and remains the most sophisticated form of communication between the educated rider and the commensurately schooled horse.

It comprises a bradoon, a light jointed snaffle with either small rings or a small eggbutt cheek, and a curb bit to which is attached a curb chain, kept in place by a lipstrap. The curb bit is fastened to the cheekpieces of the bridle, while the bradoon, fitted in the mouth above the curb bit, is suspended from a sliphead.

Variations occur in the diameter of the curb's mouthpiece and in the shape of the ports, the curve in the centre of the mouthpiece, and at least one incorporates a roller set into the port following the patterns made popular during the Renaissance. The advantage of that particular arrangement is, however, questionable. The German-type curbs are fitted almost entirely with thick, broad mouthpieces, but many bits, particularly the British ones, are still made with the traditional **Cambridge** mouth, which is far lighter. The length of the cheek is also subject

A bradoon frequently used in a double bridle. It is named a Cambridge bradoon

Right: A show hunter in a well-fitting bridle employing a Banbury curb bit. In this instance the bradoon rein is being carried outside of the little finger

BITS AND BITTING

to variation, the very short cheek of 3½in (89mm), allowing minimal leverage, being called a **Tom Thumb**. Modern thinking makes little or no distinction between the length of cheek *below* and *above* the mouthpiece, although these, as well as the cheeks' length in relation to the mouthpiece, are matters of

some consequence in the action and in what may be termed the *balance of leverage*.

Nonetheless, the principal difference is between the curb bit with a *slide-* or *turn-cheek* allowing about a ½in (13mm) movement of the mouthpiece, and the *fixed* cheek curb. Correctly, the former is a **Ward**

75

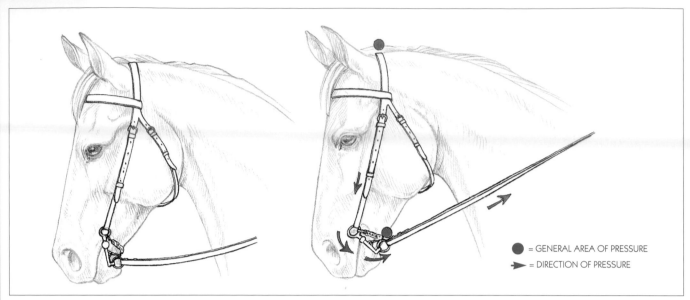

= GENERAL AREA OF PRESSURE

= DIRECTION OF PRESSURE

Above: The diagram shows the complex action of the curb bit by which flexion is induced at the poll

Union and the latter a **Weymouth**. Thankfully, Leicester curbs, Meltons, Dick Christians, Thurlows, Chifneys, Harry Highovers, and so on are no longer relevant. (One dreads to think what heinous misattributions the catalogue compilers would have committed with that lot.)

ACTION

In basic terms, the bradoon acts to raise the head, should it be necessary to correct the carriage. The curb bit, employing a simple system of levers, causes flexion at the poll to bring the face closer to the vertical plane, as well as flexion and relaxation in the lower jaw that prevents the horse poking the nose in advance of the vertical.

A well known horseman of days now gone used to describe the double bridle as having an 'up and in effect', an economical and succinct definition if ever there was one. The *bradoon* in this context acts upwards on the corners of the lips. The *curb*, however, is altogether more complex and involves pressures on almost every part of the head involved in bitting.

When the curb is at an angle of 45 degrees in the mouth, as a result of rein action, the part of the cheek above the mouthpiece that incorporates the eye to which the bridle cheekpiece is attached, moves forward on its permitted arc. In doing so it pulls downwards on the bridle cheek, a pressure which as a result is transmitted through the headpiece to the poll and exerts a lowering effect as a balance against the opposite action of the bradoon.

NOTE: The angle at which the bit is brought into play depends upon the adjustment of the *curb chain*. If it is fitted to lie very snugly on the curb groove, the bit comes into action earlier than the quoted 45 degrees that is generally considered usual and the poll pressure is commensurately less. In effect, therefore, poll pressure and, indeed, the flexion of the poll are closely related to the adjustment of the curb chain — given, of course, that the rider is sufficiently sensitive in applying and controlling the rein pressures with the fingers.

The tightened curb chain in conjunction with the action of the mouthpiece encourages a relaxation (flexion) of the lower jaw and a corresponding retraction of the nose.

According to the conformation of the mouth and the dimensions of the port, the mouthpiece puts pressure across the tongue and bars, the effect being downwards and to the rear.

Just how great or otherwise is the intensity of the

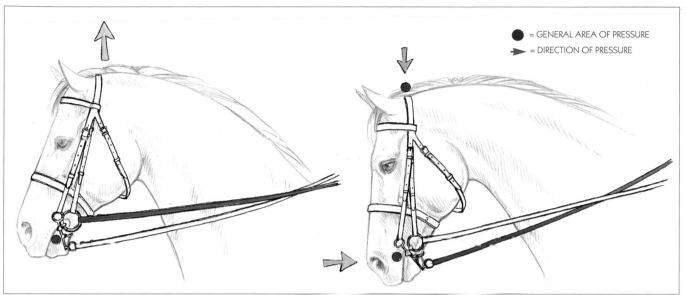

● = GENERAL AREA OF PRESSURE
➤ = DIRECTION OF PRESSURE

The 'up and in' effect of bradoon and curb, left and right respectively

pressure depends certainly on the manner in which the hand is applied, and also on the bit's construction/design, matters that should take into account the conformation of the mouth. The potential severity of the bit is concerned with:

1 The length of the cheek, overall and above and below the mouthpiece
2 The adjustment of the curb chain (loosely adjusted the curb has the ability to increase the severity of the overall action)
3 The shape of the ported mouthpiece

The degree of possible poll pressure increases or decreases according to the length of the cheek above the mouthpiece.

IDEAL MEASUREMENTS
The principle of levers is best met, and the bit will avoid causing discomfort, when the length of cheek above the mouthpiece is 1¾in (44mm) and when the cheek below the mouthpiece is twice the length of the upper one, ie 3½in (89mm): thus the overall length will be 5¼in (133mm).

Most production bits follow the rule of thumb that calls for the length of cheek to equal the width of the mouthpiece. Usually it works, but of course, it ignores entirely any individual requirements. For example, a

percentage of horses resent poll pressure, and to accommodate them the length of cheek, particularly that above the mouthpiece, should, therefore, be shorter. Indeed, it is unlikely that the upper cheek should ever be longer than the recommended length.

Almost to a man, the older school of horsemen condemned poll pressure, regarding the actions of the bradoon and headpiece as being an exercise in opposing forces and therefore both illogical and unnecessary. Whilst accepting minimal poll pressure as being unavoidable, they considered its deliberate imposition to be contrary to the pure principles of working from the relaxation of the lower jaw, and to be detrimental to the lightness of hand that they regarded as the ultimate goal.

A cheek longer than 3½in (89mm) below the mouthpiece will obviously increase the possible leverage, and there is the risk of the mouth being damaged if the hands at the end of the rein are less than supremely sensitive.

The shorter, Tom Thumb-type cheek operates with less leverage, but may be more suitable for the very sensitive mouth. Inevitably, however, there is a loss of action. The bit may satisfy humane sentiments, but it may be that it does so at the cost of an effective result.

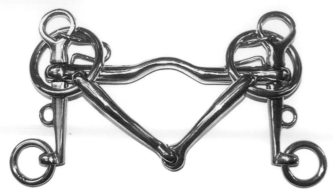

The short cheek of the Tom Thumb curb reduces the possible leverage that can be exerted and is thought to be the most suitable for a very sensitive mouth

It is obvious that the more closely fitting the curb chain, the less will be the rein tension necessary to produce an action on the bars, tongue and curb groove. But the length of the upper cheek is in itself critical to the fitting of the curb chain, for the reason that the eye of the upper cheek carries the curb hooks to which the curb chain is fastened. It needs to be just long enough to draw the chain into the curb groove when the rein is applied. If it is too long the chain is pulled too much upwards, out of the groove and onto the unprotected jaw bones, and there is no surer way of causing the horse to poke his nose in an act of understandable resistance. Of course, too loose a curb chain is just as bad, for it, too, will rise up out of the curb groove to chafe the jaw bones.

Usually a curb chain, excluding the hooks, will be satisfactory when it is about 25 per cent longer than the width of the mouthpiece.

RULE OF THE PORT

The port in the mouthpiece is critical to the action of the curb and, also, to the horse's acceptance of it. The shape of the port – correctly the tongue port, for its purpose is to accommodate that organ – governs the pressure placed upon both bars and tongue. A very shallow port, or a mullen mouthpiece, bears more upon the tongue than the bars of the mouth. A deeper port encourages the tongue to be raised into it and allows the mouthpiece to bear more directly on the bars.

Very high ports are fortunately rare. If they are sufficiently high it is quite possible for them to come into contact with the roof of the mouth. In some parts of the world that would be acceptable and even desirable, but the practice has no place in European riding.

The golden rule, in days when the subject of bitting embraced both precision and accuracy and was given the most meticulous attention, was that the width of the port should equal that of the tongue groove or channel, ie the space under the tongue enclosed on either side by the bars. If it was too narrow it would not allow sufficient room for the tongue, if too wide it would prevent there being enough bearing on the bars.

By experiment and by long observation of many hundreds, perhaps thousands of mouths, the consensus was that the desirable width suiting almost every horse was 1⅓in (34mm), that measurement being based on the assumption (a very well supported one) that the width of the channel is in most instances three-quarters the height of the bars, the latter being taken to be 1⅘in (46mm). (One has to reflect that scarcely one in ten of the modern riding population appreciate the significance of the tongue groove, and may indeed never even have heard of it! It is nonetheless important).

SLIDE VERSUS FIXED CHEEK

Modern practice inclines towards the use of the fixed cheek as being more immediate and definite in its action. In fact, however, there are good arguments in favour of the slide cheek that are and have been made by leading authorities.

It was argued that the lightening of the curb rein when the horse had responded to the request for flexion at the poll and in the lower jaw allowed the mouthpiece to slide down the cheek thus easing the pressure on the mouth. It was held that the action constituted a reward for the horse's co-operation and compliance and was, therefore, both logical and laudable.

However, it all depends on the bit being so precisely constructed that the mouthpiece really does slide up and down smoothly and equally on both sides. If the construction does not meet those criteria then the mouthpiece will be uneven in its action and cause more trouble than it is worth.

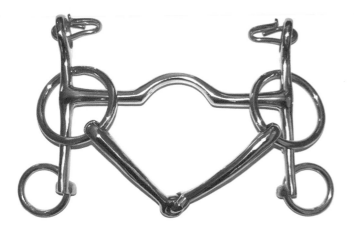

A fixed cheek curb bit which used to be known as the Ward Union

The slide, turn cheek curb bit which is, correctly, a Weymouth

A further consideration is the ability of the rider to operate the curb rein independently of the bradoon so as to achieve the desired result.

On the whole, today's bits are not made to that standard and the German manufacturers, who could make perfectly engineered slide cheeks, prefer to stick to the less complicated process involved in making the more popular fixed cheek. It is doubtful, too, whether the slide cheek has much support in current thinking and practice. That, of course, does not absolve the rider from learning how to handle the reins with a high degree of dexterity.

It might also be thought reasonable for the horse to be accustomed to the varied pressures of the curb/bradoon combination from the ground before being ridden in one.

USE OF THE REINS

Usually the bradoon rein is broader than the curb rein, but the manner in which they are held differs depending on the school of thought or, perhaps, the country to which one belongs.

The British tendency, for instance, is to hold the bradoon rein outside the little finger and outside the curb rein, which is held between the third and fourth finger. In that position it is probable that the bradoon rein is predominant. If the reins are reversed then the curb will be the more dominant of the two. The head can then be raised by the hands being turned a little

upward in a lifting action, and lowered by turning them downwards.

Elsewhere it is recommended, and probably accepted, that the bradoon is held outside the little finger but with the end of the curb rein leaving the hand through the first and second fingers and being held in place by the thumb. The thumb prevents the bradoon rein slipping through the hand, while the two middle fingers act easily to increase or release tension on the curb rein.

Whatever method is employed, the success of the double bridle depends largely on the rider's ability to

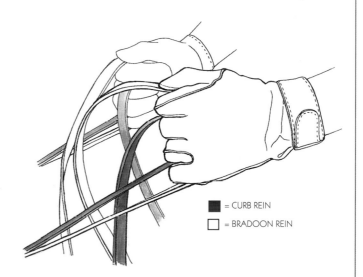

■ = CURB REIN
□ = BRADOON REIN

The reins of the double bridle held with the bradoon outside the little finger. With the reins held in this fashion the influence of the bradoon is predominant

manage the reins controlling its action. It goes without saying that only practice makes perfect – but that is true also of finger exercises for the piano!

BANBURY POWER

A notable exception to the conventional curb patterns is the **Banbury**, a bit which is frequently effective when others are causing problems. It has a straight-bar mouthpiece tapered at the centre but by no means allowing as much room for the tongue as the usual port. The cheeks are slotted to allow the mouthpiece to revolve in the mouth and to move up and down. It is, therefore, loose in the mouth and can be 'mouthed' to cause salivation. Quite importantly, the arrangement prevents the horse taking hold of the bit and clamping it firmly between the jaws.

It is difficult to see how any pressure can be brought to bear directly over the bars, and that may be one of the reasons why it seems to be acceptable to horses which react unfavourably to the conventional mouthpiece.

Since the cheeks are capable of rotation it is possible to operate each one independently – an advantage with a horse who resists by stiffening one or other side of the mouth and one that allows a great variation in the bit action.

To ride successfully with a double bridle of any pattern it is absolutely essential for the rider to appreciate the need to strike a balance between the diverse actions of the bit and bradoon, melding the two into a harmonious whole. When that happy state is attained it is possible, on a horse schooled to respond to the indications of the bridle, to obtain improved balance, outline and movement with a degree of finesse impossible with any other bitting arrangement.

CURB CHAINS

As we have seen, the curb chain acts on the curb groove as an integral part of the system of levers, encouraging the jaw to relax and the nose to be retracted. It is entirely critical to the action of the bit and the overall success of the double bridle, and as such, it deserves meticulous attention in its choice and fitting.

Chains are made from linked metal rings. They can be single links or double ones to provide continuous smooth mesh, or they can be made with broader, flat links. The last two are always the most satisfactory and are certainly less likely to cause irritation.

The chain can be softened in its action by fitting a **rubber curb guard,** which will also prevent chafing. However, if it is thought necessary to use a rubber guard it is well worth considering a leather curb or even an elastic one.

Neatly finished **leather curbs** with three links on either end for fastening to the curb hooks are effective and comfortable (so long as they are kept clean, soft and supple): they are also expensive. Just as good (and probably better, too) is a shaped strip of soft **red,**

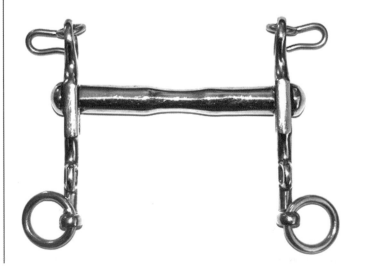

The lesser known Banbury curb bit is nonetheless a very effective pattern. The cheeks rotate independently which can be an advantage with a horse that stiffens his mouth on one side

Single and double link curb chains. The latter is deemed to be more satisfactory

Rubber curb guard used to prevent chafing and in the general interest of the horse's comfort

buffalo hide of pre-determined length made with a slit at either end to fasten over the curb hooks, or there is the doubled **elastic curb**, which is very good.

These three curb straps can be fitted very snugly without the risk of causing discomfort, and the resilience of the elastic pattern is an additional and particular bonus.

Whatever curb is employed, it has to be fitted with a central fly link to accommodate the **lipstrap**, without which no double bridle is complete. Fastened to

A leather curb chain, if kept soft, is comfortable and for that reason very effective. The elastic curb (below) is probably even better because of its resilience

the 'loops' on the cheeks, supplied for that purpose, it prevents the curb rising out of the curb groove and bearing on the thinly covered jaw bones. (It will also prevent the bit from ever becoming reversed in the mouth, an unlikely happening but not impossible. If

The Jodhpur polo curb which is fitted snugly between the jaw bones

and when it occurs the result may be very unpleasant indeed.)

CURB HOOKS

The hooks to which the curb chain is attached are secured to the eye of the cheek and can be regarded as the Achilles heel of the curb bit. Frequently they are poorly made, and can be a source of discomfort and chafing. It is true that as many problems occur in the use of the double bridle on account of cheap curb hooks as on any other account.

The German-made hooks and those on the best quality English bits are much better than the usual run of Far Eastern imports and are generally acceptable. Nonetheless, the best of all is the flat **circle curb hook**. It lies absolutely flat and will rarely cause chafing to the sensitive skin around the corners of the lips.

The circle curb hook can lie absolutely flat and will rarely be the cause of chafing

FITTING

Curb chains should be a close and snug fit. It is a mistaken kindness for them to be adjusted loosely, because they can then ride up out of the groove and chafe the jaw bones: quite apart from the discomfort caused, the action of the bit is then more or less seriously impaired.

Left: The interesting Icelandic 'curb' bit, capable of exerting considerable pressures on the poll and the lower jaw without, thankfully, the employment of a curb chain. It is not dissimilar to some patterns of the mis-named American gag

Right: Shades of Juan Segundo and his system of bitting for cavalry. This cleverly engineered interchangeable mouthpiece set is made by the German firm of Sprenger

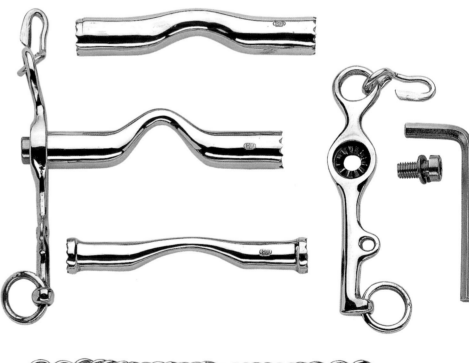

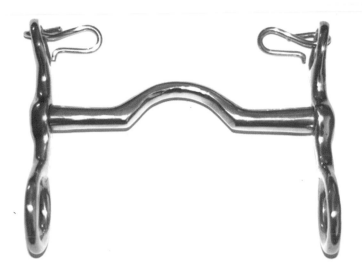

Right: The Hunloke curb bit, sometimes termed Globe Cheek Pelham, which it is not. The cheek is short and it can be a useful bit for show ponies

Left: This German bit, described as a 'Pony Bradoon with cheek bar' harks back to the driving bridle of the heavy horse or the 'watering' bridle of a previous era, which allowed easy release of the bit. It is not relevant to modern equitation

Right: Bradoon with shaped spatula

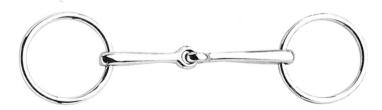

Left: Bradoon with lightweight jointed mouthpiece

Right: Bradoon with a heavier, rounded mouthpiece

Left: A fixed cheek curb bit with the eyes properly inclined outward to avoid chafing. The elegant S-shape cheek is more usually associated with military bits, but it is also used in the show-ring when a hack may be exhibited on a single curb bit of this design

Right: A straight forward curb bit with a shallow port giving greater bearing on the tongue. The quality is exceptional

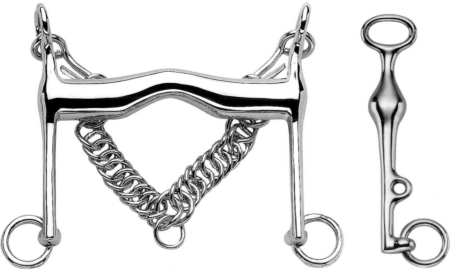

Left: A curb bit constructed with a hollow mouth so as to reduce the weight

Left: A generous port, removing the possibly irritating pressure on the tongue, is a feature of this German 'Special Dressage Bit'

Right: The mouthpiece of this bit makes a conscious and intelligent attempt to conform to the anatomy of the mouth, the port being inclined forward. However, it is a bit only for the more advanced horse

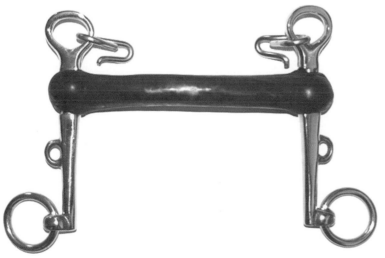

Left: An old-fashioned vulcanite or rubber mullen mouth – soft, comfortable and not too pronounced in its action

THE PELHAM

Essentially the Pelham is about one mouth-piece, a curb chain and two pairs of reins combining the action of the double bridle and attempting to achieve the same result as the combination of bradoon and curb bit.

For some people it is an appealing compromise, less demanding of horse and rider than the double bridle. It is possible to criticise the Pelham group on a variety of counts and to argue that it cannot by virtue of its design approach the sophisticated action of the double bridle. That is certainly true, but then neither can the snaffle take the place of the double bridle. It should, I think, be regarded as a bitting arrangement in its own right, a useful half-way house that suits a number of horses and riders. On the other hand, it has also to be recognised that there are some very unintelligent patterns – the jointed

Left: An eggbutt cheek Pelham used with a rounding joining the snaffle and curb rings. The bit is then reduced to a 'bland, blunt instrument' but is nonetheless effective

mouth Pelham, for example – and that confusion can arise in respect of the action as a result of the family of multi-ring bits, variously described as gags, that do not employ a curb chain but are in all other essentials a Pelham bit when employed with two reins. With a single rein on the lowest ring the bit exerts the action of a curb, more or less. The attraction of what may almost be regarded as a sixth bitting group is that with the rein on the main mouthpiece ring, the action is that of the snaffle – allowing, that is, a certain difference brought about by the additional ring to which the bridle cheek is fastened. It can, therefore, be used to fulfil three functions. What it does *not* do is to emulate the action of a gag!

ACTION

If the top rein were to be used independently, the action of the Pelham resembles the upward one of the snaffle, allowing for the angles at which the face is

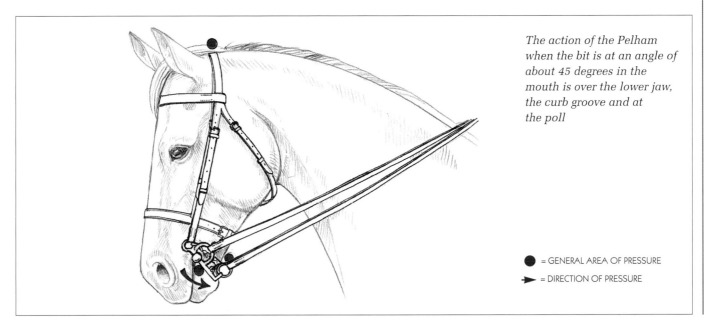

The action of the Pelham when the bit is at an angle of about 45 degrees in the mouth is over the lower jaw, the curb groove and at the poll

● = GENERAL AREA OF PRESSURE

➤ = DIRECTION OF PRESSURE

held in relation to the body. If the bottom rein is employed we have curb action. If both reins are held in the hand, the action, it must be presumed, is somewhere between the two. The play of the fingers and, more particularly, of the wrists allows for *some* predominance of one or other effect, but not to the extent possible with the double bridle. (In times past, when more emphasis was put on the Pelham as well as considerable ingenuity expended on its design, a nagsman schooling a young horse would often use the bit with the reins being held in separate hands in order to balance the effect of snaffle and curb action.)

That is possibly too simplistic a view, since the basic action is subject also to the mouthpiece involved, and there are a great many of them, some being more productive than others.

DISADVANTAGES

Because of its construction, largely in relation to the fitting of the curb, the bit can chafe the lips and corners of the mouth if it is fitted high enough to be effective. Even more importantly, the cheek above the mouthpiece has to be made longer to accommodate the bradoon ring. Very often it is made too long and so accentuates the possible poll pressure as well as contributing to the difficulty of fitting the bit correctly. The problem will be further compounded if the eyes of the bit are not shaped *outwards* to prevent their rubbing against the face.

There is a further failing to the Pelham if one is concerned with national or international dressage riding – in short, it is not permitted. (The Pelham is allowed in the dressage phase of Pony Club Junior Horse Trials, however.)

ADVANTAGES

If in theory the Pelham *should* be an ineffective bitting arrangement, it is not so in practice and many horses go very happily in it. It is possible that they do so because the action is soft, imprecise and not too demanding, and for that reason it is useful when dealing with a horse who has lost confidence because of a damaged mouth.

Moreover, a Pelham is usually better suited to horses with short, thick jaw formations that have difficulty in coping with the bit and bradoon of the double bridle. Such a jaw formation is usually associated with the thickset, cobby sort of animal but the Pelham is sometimes the better bit for an Arab, too.

Conversely, the Pelham is not at all suitable for long-jawed Thoroughbred types, when the bit, if it is placed high enough to be any good, causes the curb chain to rise up out of the curb groove and rest against the thinly covered jaw bones.

DIVISIONS

The principle divisions in the Pelham mouthpieces are between the conventional **mullen** mouthpiece, frequently in vulcanite, or sometimes in flexible rubber, nylon or a similar plastic; the **ported** mouthpiece, correctly named Hartwell but frequently termed Cambridge; the more mechanically efficient **arch-mouth**; and the very unintelligent **jointed** mouthpiece.

The first is a soft mouthpiece resting on the tongue with little or no pressure being exerted directly on the bars in response to the use of the curb rein.

The mildest form of Pelham is probably that fitted with a mullen (half-moon) mouthpiece of vulcanite. It is a bit in common use

The ported mouthpiece allows for more pressure on the bars, as in the curb bit, and the upward curve of the arch-mouth ensures that it does indeed rest over the bars.

The jointed mouthpiece makes very much less

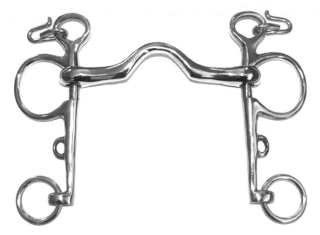

The Hartwell or ported mouth used with Pelham cheeks is one of the most effective of this group, permitting a degree of pressure on the bars of the mouth

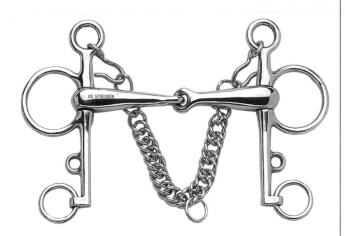

The most unintelligent of the Pelham groups is that fitted with a jointed mouthpiece which will negate any curb action

A sub-division can be made between an eggbutt and a slide cheek, but in the Pelham it is not a matter of much consequence.

SOME NOTABLE PATTERNS

The **Hanoverian** Pelham, once much used as a polo bit as well as for children's show ponies, appears to work rather well in the 'stronger' category. It is notable for a central port, jointed on either side, and for the rollers set round the mouth.

The arch-mouth Pelham (Mors l'Hotte) allows additional room for the tongue and so acts more efficiently on the bars

sense. Inevitably it squeezes the cheeks as the 'nutcracker' action is induced, and it is difficult to see what accepted curb action is possible. If there is to be any action, however debased, it is essential for the curb chain to be passed through the top rein loop, which is the case with most Pelhams – with notable exceptions like the S. M. (Sam Marsh) and the Rugby.

Without this adjustment the curb chain falls out of the curb groove when the mouthpiece assumes a V-shape in the mouth. The same occurs, of course, when an India rubber or flexible mouth is used, but to a lesser degree.

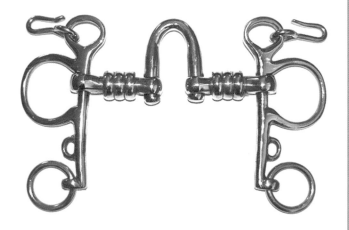

The Hanoverian Pelham, jointed on either side of the port, is a stronger bit and was once a popular form of bitting for polo

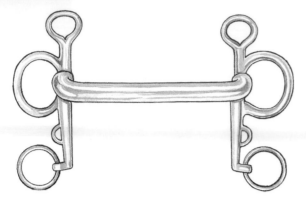

The turned back mouthpiece of the Scamperdale prevents chafing of the lips but presents a problem in the correct fitting of the curb-chain

The **Scamperdale**, named after the establishment made famous by the late Sam Marsh, a noted horseman and trainer up to and just after World War II, seeks to obviate the tendency towards chafing the lips and corners of the mouth – a common failing of the Pelham group – by turning back the mouthpiece at either end so that those areas are avoided. It succeeds, but it causes problems with the fitting of the curb chain.

Excluding the **Army Universal** or angle-cheek, which has to be accepted as a practical bitting arrangement and well proven in view of its use on large numbers of horses by horsemen of no more than

average ability, the two most effective Pelhams are the **S.M. (Sam Marsh)**, sometimes called the Faudel-Phillips, and the **Rugby**. Possibly one might make up a trio with the inclusion of the Banbury mouth made up with a Pelham cheek.

Sam Marsh and Faudel-Phillips, another pre-war horseman of note, both used the Pelham which bears one or other of their names with some success, and it is an entirely intelligent bit. (In fact, whilst both gentlemen were responsible for its popularity in Britain, it originated in the United States and was introduced to the British market by the Distas Saddlery Company in the 1930s when Pelhams were very much in vogue.)

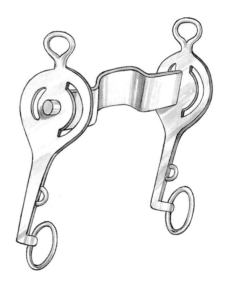

One of the most effective Pelham patterns is the S.M. (Sam Marsh). It features a broad, flat-ported mouthpiece and the cheeks move independently on a limited arc

The cheeks of the S.M. move independently on a restricted arc, while the broad, flat-ported mouthpiece gives wide, comfortable coverage over the bars and, if properly used, will encourage flexion at both poll and lower jaw.

The Rugby, taking its name from the British town in Warwickshire which was once an important centre for British polo, is now frequently, and quite shamelessly, referred to in at least one bitting catalogue as a 'false Weymouth'. It is notable for the independently linked bradoon ring which allows for the curb chain to be fitted in the normal manner. The bit can be made with a plain mouth, a ported one, which is perhaps the most effective, or sometimes with rollers set round the mouthpiece.

It is closer to the curb bit in character, allows more

The Army Universal is a practical uniform bitting arrangement for large bodies of horses, allowing alternative fittings according to individual need

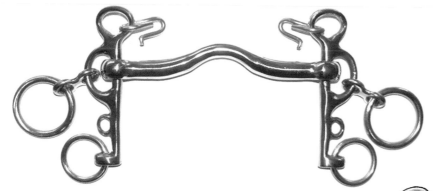

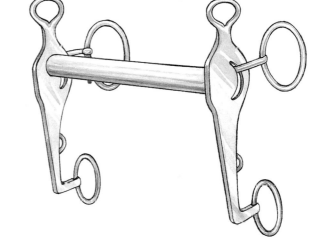

Left: The ported Rugby Pelham (the 'Weymouth look-alike') is closer to the curb-bit in character and whilst being a useful polo bit can also be used to effect an introduction to the double bridle

Below: A variation on the Rugby which retains the independent bradoon link but employs the less demanding mullen mouthpiece

clearly defined curb pressure, and exerts some action on the poll. As well as being a useful polo bit it could, and can, be used as an introduction to the double bridle, accustoming the horse to the curb action.

A popular member of the Pelham group is the **Kimblewick**, an adaptation of a Spanish-pattern jumping bit. (The bit is named after the Buckinghamshire village where Phil Oliver lived. He was father of the showjumper and course-builder Alan Oliver, and it was he who introduced the bit to Britain and the international jumping circuit.) Its action, firmly in the Pelham mode, is a combination of snaffle and curb, inclining more to the latter. A feature of the true

Kimblewick is the square eye to which the bridle cheek is fastened. It allows for poll pressure and was integral to the original pattern. Today, it is often made with a rounded eye, probably because manufacturers are unaware of the purpose of the squared eye.

To fulfil the concept of the bit the mouthpiece, either of metal or vulcanite, should be ported to allow for pressure over the bars. A mullen mouth blurs the action of the bit by bearing on the tongue, and a jointed mouth is a nonsense.

On the whole, it is satisfactory enough for the curb chain to be fitted in the usual way, but the action will be strengthened considerably if the chain passes through the rein ring.

The object of the Kimblewick is to give more or less instant control to the rider by causing the head

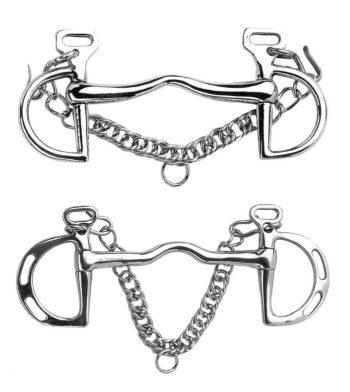

Left: Two Kimblewick patterns. The top one is a true Kimblewick, the one below has a rounded eye, reducing poll pressure, and the slots in the cheek allow an alternative in the rein position which effectively fixes the action

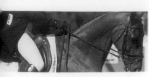

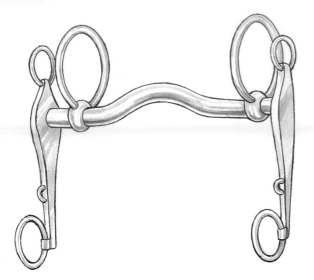

Left: Swales 3 in 1 is a severe bit employing an uncomfortable squeezing action of the inside rings. On the whole, horses would be better off without it

Right: A Pelham fitted with a cleverly shaped, resilient 'Happy Mouth'. It is commonly available in America but the design of this well-constructed bit is nonetheless flawed. The eye is set too far to the rear and affects the action of the curb chain

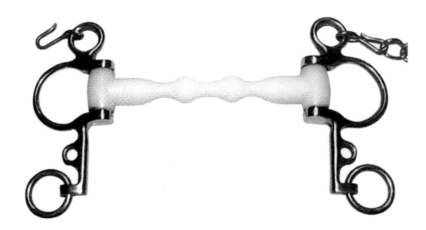

Left: In fact this is no more than a multi-ring snaffle since no curb action is involved. With the rein on the lower ring, considerable poll pressure is obtained and it would be possible to use the bit with two reins. Whilst not a logical concept it is in popular use. It is, however, NOT A GAG, whatever the name given to it

to be lowered and, in consequence, the mouth to be carried lower than the hand – a prime requisite in obtaining control. It is achieved by the rein slipping a little down the ring in response to a lowered hand. The effect then is to produce a direct poll and curb pressure, the latter via the chain, combined with a pretty strong downward pressure on or over the bars of the mouth. It is the lowered hand, however, that is essential to the effective operation of the bit.

The bit can, nonetheless, cause problems in the wrong hands. Over-employed, the horse begins to hang on the bit and the hands and it is possible for bruising to occur on the lips, bars and the edges of the tongue.

In the right hands it is a good 'change' bit for an impetuous subject and becomes salutary in its effect when used in conjunction with a running martingale. It will 'stop' a strong pony, but on the whole it is not a bit suitable for children, whose lack of security is frequently made manifest by very rough hands.

ROUNDINGS AND REINS

Leather roundings, joining the curb and bradoon rings, allow the rider to use a single rein, but they significantly compromise any constructive bit action, reducing the Pelham to a bland and blunt instrument.

An adjustable divided rein, fitted to give some curb action, is better, but it, too, has its failings, although it can be useful for small children.

The usual pattern of 'rounding' used to join snaffle and curb ring to allow the use of a single rein

The adjustable divided rein is more mechanically efficient, although it precludes the use of a running martingale

CHAPTER 4

GAG BITS

The dictionary definitions of the word 'gag' are numerous, and range from retching and strangulation to the music hall joke. Nonetheless, they also include a definition to cover the equestrian context: '... a powerful bit used for breaking horses', and then, more accurately, 'a rein passing through a gag runner *so as to draw the bit upward in the horse's mouth*'. The italics are mine. The distinguished lexicographers may be a shade confused, like the compilers of the modern bit catalogues, but they are correct about the bit being drawn 'upward in the horse's mouth'.

Disregarding the exercise in semantics that has resulted in multi-ring snaffle-cum-curb bits being designated as gags – Dutch, American or otherwise – a gag may properly and very simply be defined as a bit which, by virtue of the construction of the rings, accentuates the upward, lifting action of the snaffle against the corners of the mouth.

The gag would seem to originate in the bearing, or overcheck, reins much used on the driving horse in the Victorian era to give a high, flashy head carriage. Anna Sewell, the author of *Black Beauty*, campaigned tirelessly against their use, and there is little doubt that in the late nineteenth century the tight, fixed adjustment of the bearing rein amounted to an unacceptable cruelty.

The gag bit used on the riding horse is by no means so severe since it does not arbitrarily fix the head position, its action being governed by the rider's hand. Its severity, one might say, is in direct ratio to the competence of the rider – and that, in some instances, may give rise to some concern.

Nonetheless, it serves a useful purpose in modern competitive sports and sometimes in the hunting field, whilst its use in the sport of polo is almost universal.

ACTION

The primary action of the conventional gag bit depends upon the holes set top and bottom of the bit rings and the cheekpiece of rounded leather or cord that passes through them and to which the rein is attached. In swift response to rein pressure the rounding slides through the holes in the bit rings and raises the bit upwards in the mouth, giving a clear indication to the horse that it should lift the head, whilst at the same time it exerts some pressure against the mouth to bring the nose inwards. In the interests of self-preservation, such an action is not unreasonable if one is riding a strong-pulling horse who persists in approaching his fences with his head carried between his knees, nor is it other than a sensible practice to use a gag to encourage a horse (in conjunction with active legs, of course) to lift his head rather than to persist in hanging downward on the hand.

The old school of nagsman would often use what was known as a 'hack overcheck' with a curb bit to establish an acceptable elevated head carriage. The 'overcheck' was fitted with a light 'wire' mouthpiece to very small gag rings.

In some instances the mouthpiece was a twisted one which would have an even more salutary action. Of course, such an item had to be used with care by good, skilful hands if the arrangement was to operate effectively – but then, the old nagsman was rarely deficient in that department.

Used in that context, the overcheck was a training

Right: A gag bridle used on an event horse to give a greater measure of control

quite legitimate restraint for the big, highly couraged, galloping horse, whose rider may often be a light-weight young lady.

In both cases the strong *secondary* action of the bridle is involved in the degree and nature of the control exerted.

It follows that if the bit applies an upward pressure in the mouth as a result of rein action, a corresponding pressure will be applied to the poll through the bridle head to which the cheeks are attached. There is then a sort of both-ends-against-the-middle situation. The severity of the action will be made more so if the gag is used in conjunction with a standing martingale, which, to some degree prevents the horse escaping the pressures by raising its head. The employment of a standing martingal is to all intents universal on the polo ground and in conjunction with a gag bit constitutes a most powerful control system. In eventing the Martingale is not in evidence, although the gag will be supported by a noseband of one pattern or author which closes the mouth and puts some restraining pressure on the nose to discourage the head from being thrown upwards.

TYPES AND CONSTRUCTION

Any mouthpiece can be fitted with gag rings, either loose rings passing through holes in the butt-end of the mouthpiece, or fixed eggbutt-type rings like those employed in what is rightly termed the Cheltenham gag. It is claimed that the eggbutt ring is more effective since this allows the mouthpiece to drop more easily when the pressure on the rein is released. Nonetheless, the loose ring, particularly if it is a large one, is the more popular. The large ring,

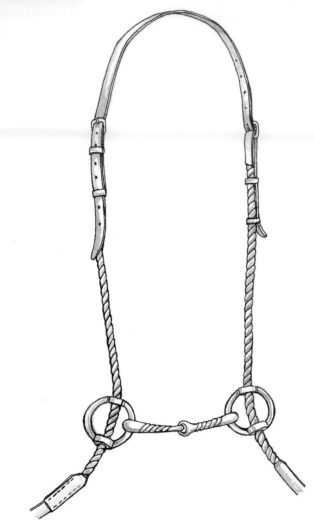

The hack 'over-check', derived from the bearing rein, can be used in conjunction with a curb bit to establish an appropriate head carriage – but only by competent horsemen!

aid and *not* an instrument designed to increase the physical control of the horse. One would be chary of recommending its use to any but the most gifted of modern riders.

Conversely, the gag is used purely as a system of control on the polo field, and a pretty powerful one at that. It ensures by the application of coercive mechanics the swift responses necessarily demanded by the game. (Alas, the days of the polo greats who rode for the most part with lowered hand in double bridles or Pelhams supported by a standing martingale have long since gone.)

The gag is also used in the sport of eventing as a

A Cheltenham gag employs a fixed, eggbutt cheek which, it is thought, allows the bit to drop in the mouth more easily

A cherry-roller gag, once called a Rodzianko. The presence of rollers discourage a horse from bearing down on the hand

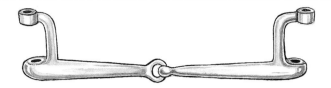

The Duncan gag evolved specifically for use with a curb bit. The attenuated cheek makes it particularly suitable for this purpose

of course, is in contact with a large area of the cheeks and will help to reinforce directional changes as well as adding to the overall strength of the action.

A gag still in frequent use is that which incorporates rollers round the mouthpiece. It is held that the rollers discourage the horse from bearing heavily on the hand or from setting its jaw against the mouthpiece. This bit, while being an old pattern, used to be known as Colonel Rodzianko's gag after one of the greatest of showjumping trainers. (Paul Rodzianko was a member of the crack Russian jumping team of pre-World War I days which won the 1913 Nations Cup at London's International Horse Show. After the Revolution, Rodzianko came to Britain where he ran a notable training centre. He was responsible for the success of

the great Irish jumping teams which won no less than twenty-three Nations Cups between 1928 and 1939.)

The practice of naming a bit after some exceptional horseman or trainer who popularised its use was prevalent in the years before and immediately after World War II. The Magenis snaffle, often called 'Talbot-Ponsonby's' bit, is an example. In fact, of course, Magenis is a corruption of McGuiness, a noted Leicestershire hunting man of the nineteenth century.

Polo players have also used Pelham bits fitted with a gag-type top ring, whilst the Duncan gag was designed specifically for use with the curb bit of a double bridle. Then there is the Hitchcock gag, produced by the American expert after whom it is named. The design ensures maximum elevatory

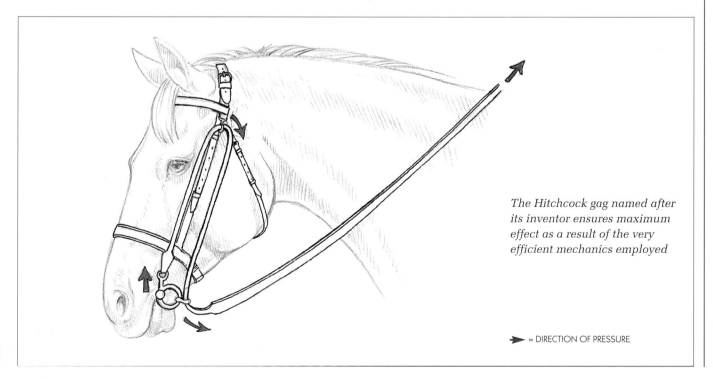

The Hitchcock gag named after its inventor ensures maximum effect as a result of the very efficient mechanics employed

➤ = DIRECTION OF PRESSURE

BITS AND BITTING

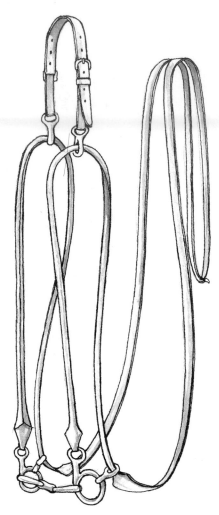

Detail of the Hitchcock gag revealing some affinity with the overcheeks used on the driving horse

power combined with extraordinary speed of operation, whilst delivering a powerful, and contradictory, downward poll pressure. It makes use of a pulley arrangement, one pulley fitted at the bit ring and one on the bridle head in a development of a system employed with overchecks used in harness work. Otherwise, one might think that its action was akin to placing the horse's head in a vice.

The cheekpieces of the gag bridle, which slide through the holes in the rings, can be made of 'rounded' leather, made by stitching the leather round a cord; or from a strip of rawhide; or, which is probably the most satisfactory, they can be made from cord alone. Whatever the material, it is advisable for the cheeks to be kept greased to facilitate the sliding action.

Ideally the cheek should be fitted with a leather or metal 'stop' to limit the upward action of the bit. An extra rein, fastened to the bit ring in the usual way is a sensible addition to the gag bridle, allowing the gag rein to be brought into play as necessary, when it will be found to be more effective than when the upward gag action is continual.

Of course, the gag is an example of mechanical means used to produce a strong system of control, but, obviously, it has its place in certain circumstances. What is absolutely certain is that the family of gag bridles has nothing in common with 'American' or 'Dutch' snaffles that are often called gags.

CHAPTER 5

NOSE OR BITLESS BRIDLE

The bitless or nose bridle, often termed a hackamore, with which it is so frequently confused, derives from the nose-to-bit system of the Iberian horsemen in which the horse was schooled initially, and the mouth 'made', through pressure exerted on the nose. The early classical Masters of the Renaissance did much the same thing using a cavesson.

The theory, and the practice, involves the gradual transference of control from the noseband to a potentially severe bit. This, of course, is the basis of the hackamore system discussed in chapter 8, 'Western Bitting and the Hackamore System'.

The Californian reinsman inherited the horse-lore of Iberia from the sixteenth century *conquistadores* who re-established the horse on the American continent and brought with them to the New World their methods of schooling and their equipment. The Western horseman adapted and extended both to suit his particular purpose, and whilst using the Iberian base, developed his own school of horsemanship to which the highly sophisticated hackamore system is central.

The remarkable variety of American nose bridles are offshoots of the hackamore system and, indeed, are listed as *hackamores* in the glossy American catalogues. It is not unreasonable to deplore the confusing etymology, but it has to be acknowledged that the nose bridle is just as much an all-American product as pumpkin pie or the Quarter Horse.

In a small way Europe has adopted the nose bridle. Quite often it is worn by showjumpers and at least one pattern is actually listed as a *German hackamore*, for no better reason than it is used by a prominent German rider. Increasingly, too, the nose bridle is becoming

The type of 'hackamore', in itself a misnomer, which is frequently called a 'German hackamore', for no better reason than being used by a distinguished German horseman. It is, in fact, an all-American product

99

part of endurance riders' equipment, and it is certainly well suited to an activity that demands a naturally balanced horse but is not concerned with the animal being 'on the bit' and in a state of collection.

There are, of course, a few British patterns of nose bridle, the short-cheeked W.S. Pelham (which has two reins) and its derivatives being an example. (W.S. are the initials of the late William Stone who for many

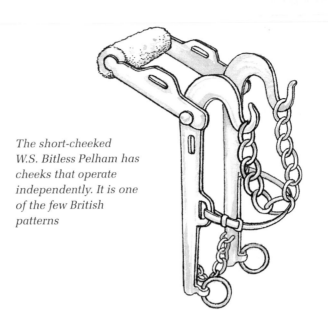

The short-cheeked W.S. Bitless Pelham has cheeks that operate independently. It is one of the few British patterns

years worked as a bit-maker with the Walsall firm of Matthew Harvey Ltd, at that time the foremost bit-makers in Europe and, indeed, the world.)

In fact, a simple form of bitless bridle can be made from a stout drop noseband with a couple of rings fitted to carry the reins. Such a bridle is surprisingly effective and is a useful piece of training equipment when teaching jumping to novice riders, for instance.

ACTION

In all patterns of the true nose bridle, control is obtained primarily through direct pressure on the nose induced by simple leverage, but in some instances curb action is also involved and in some patterns there may be a degree of poll pressure, too. The strength of the action depends on the length of the cheek, and in most instances this is sufficient to constitute a powerful means of restraint.

Lateral movement of the head has usually to be made by an exaggerated outward opening of the hand. The difficulty is addressed in some American patterns by what is termed a 'side-pull' action made possible by a small ring attachment between the cheek and the nose-piece which allows the former to be pulled side-

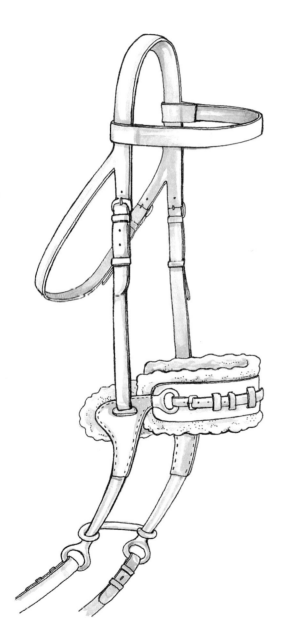

Above and left: The nose bridle known as Blair's Pattern which features an adjustable nose-piece.

The bitting arrangement shown on the opposite page might be looked upon as a prime example of kitchen-sink bitting – sponges and all!

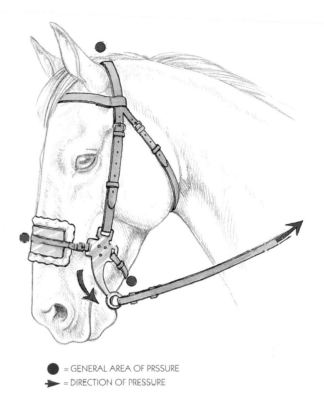

● = GENERAL AREA OF PRSSURE
→ = DIRECTION OF PRESSURE

*Above: A simple bitless bridle that is nonetheless effective.
Note the three pressure points*

ways, exerting a corresponding pull on the nose. Clearly it works, although it is still necessary to carry the hand outwards.

CONSTRUCTION

The construction of American nose bridles is extraordinarily diverse and often ingenious, but whatever the pattern, it is strong in its mechanical action — sometimes, one might think, unacceptably so. Studded nosepieces and thin curb chains operating well above the curb groove, for instance, appear unduly harsh and are certainly capable of inflicting pain when used by the heavy-handed.

The basic nose bridle comprises a nosepiece and an adjustable rear strap of leather, or more usually a chain, fitted to the cheeks. The nosepiece can be of leather, well padded with sheepskin or some other

*Left: A bitless bridle employed in the sport of tent-pegging.
The horse looks happy enough but it has not helped the rider
time his strike!*

material that will prevent chafing, and is accompanied by a similarly padded rear strap. More usually the nosepiece is a metal one covered in leather, or in some instances a bicycle chain or steel cable encased in a rubber tube. There are patterns, quite a number of them, made of plain metal rod, often tapering towards the nose, and very often the American bridles are not padded with sheepskin or anything else.

COMBINATION BRIDLES

Many of the bridles incorporate a snaffle bit, usually a pretty sharp one, and for that reason are not true nose bridles. The bit acts in conjunction with the noseband and is set on the cheeks, frequently in such a manner as to allow the bit to slide upwards in what is termed 'gag action'.

The following is an interesting description of a 'combination hackamore gag' which might with equal justification be called a 'kitchen-sink hackamore'. It is taken from an American catalogue:

'Stainless steel hackamore with twisted wire gag snaffle mouthpiece and wrapped leather steel noseband. The combination works first on the nose and then on the mouth to help a horse turn a barrel, while the sidepull action of the shank and gag tucks the nose to the inside.'

Further comment is unnecessary.

FITTING

Properly used, the nose bridle is useful and often commendable in its own right or as an alternative to the conventional bitting arrangement. However, there is no doubt of the potential to cause injury. Even with the most careful management and lots of padding it is possible to callous the nose, and an unpadded rear chain can cause chafing. If it is low enough to lie in the curb groove and can be secured in that position, then it is likely that the nosepiece will also hang too low over the nostrils.

WESTERN BITTING AND THE HACKAMORE SYSTEM

When Christopher Columbus landed in the Bahamas in 1492 on the first of his four voyages to the New World the horse had been extinct on the American continent for 8000 years or more. Yet within 400 years of that momentous landfall there were over twenty-five million horses in America, a third of the human population.

Today America still has the biggest horse population in the world. It is the most varied and arguably the most colourful. America, besides its enormous Thoroughbred industry and its hugely developed tradition of harness racing, has its own long-established 'all-American' breeds and also a unique grouping of gaited horses, the 'exotics' of the horse world, that preserve the traditions once so much prized in Europe but now lost to the Old World.

America owes its Thoroughbreds and its superlative harness racers to the early imports made from England. The harness racer, the American Standardbred, was, in fact, founded on the English Thoroughbred Messenger, a son of Mambrino, imported into the US in 1788.

The bit is a typical Western curb and potentially very severe, but the contact between hand and mouth is minimal

Both these Mexican riders have 'one-ear' bridles, whilst the horse on the left wears a lightweight bosal *with the usual curb bit*

Otherwise the predominant influence is that of the Spanish stock originally introduced to the continent by the Spanish *conquistadores*.

The Spanish settlers brought to America not only horses, but also the tradition of cattle ranching, establishing the early cattle ranges in Argentina and Mexico. They brought also the methods of schooling and riding that had been developed on the Iberian peninsula during the 700 years of the Moorish occupation, as well as their horse equipment – the saddles and the items that formed a unique system of bitting. All these survive and flourish today, if in a skilfully adapted form, in the art and culture of the Western horsemen of California and Mexico.

During the long Moorish occupation of the Iberian

peninsula, following the expansion of the Islamic empire in the seventh and eighth centuries, there evolved a system of horse schooling based on *la jaquima*, from which the word 'hackamore' is derived. It reflected an older, highly sophisticated and very skilful school of riding, and one which is just as legitimate as that with which we are familiar. In essence, indeed, it was the basis and inspiration for the classical schools in which, accepting their failings, the ultimate goal was supreme lightness in hand, a quality that is in danger of being eclipsed by modern competitive considerations.

It remains with us, at least in part, in the French school, which once pursued lightness combined with impulsion with an almost Messianic zeal. It survives in its purest form in the horsemanship of Spain and Portugal, and is still demonstrated in the art of the Californian reinsman.

The system of bitting the horse through his nose had its roots in the horsemanship of the pre-Christian

era, and whilst supreme balance, lightness and immediate response were, and still are, the goals of the Iberian horsemen, they are no more than subordinate to an essentially practical purpose.

The Iberian horse was required to perform the most advanced movements at speed – dressage at the gallop, as it were – and to do so on the weight of a looping rein attached to a high-ported curb bit and held in one hand. And, of course, it was schooled to respond immediately to the most precise distribution of the rider's weight. All were very necessary requirements in warfare and, very importantly, when working the fierce, long-horned black cattle that are still traditional to the Iberian peninsula. Indeed, it was the agile black bulls that provided the final test of the schooled horse.

In the European context the 'hackamore' is the long-cheeked bitless bridle used for the most part by showjumpers. It is, of course, also used in America, but in the original Spanish context it is a complex collection of nosebands of different weights plus a whole string of accompaniments.

Essentially, the hackamore comprises a heavy, braided rawhide noseband shaped like the solid tennis racquets of the pre-Perry era. The noseband is called, in the Spanish fashion, a *bosal* (*bosalillo*) and is made with a large, firm 'heel' knot at the rear that lies between and behind the lower jawbones.

The *bosal* is suspended from a light *latigo* headstall kept in place by a slit cut in the appropriate position so that it can be slipped over one ear. (One-ear bridles are a feature of American saddlery, and like all American tack are practical to a degree.) If necessary, the fitting is made more secure by the addition of a browband (*cavesada*).

To the all-important heel knot is attached a heavy, plaited rope rein, the *mecate*, made from mane hair.

Below: The true Western Hackamore. On the left is the heavy, braided bosal; *on the right the complete bridle:* bosal, latigo *(headstall),* fiador *(throatlatch),* mecate *(plaited rope rein) and, of course, the all-important heel knot at the rear of the* bosal

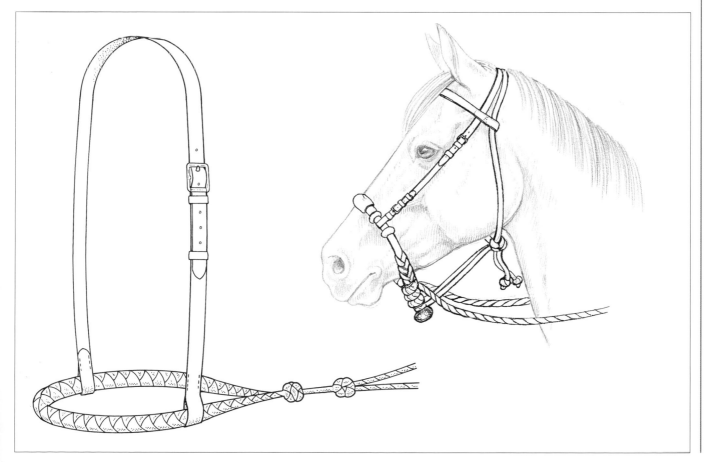

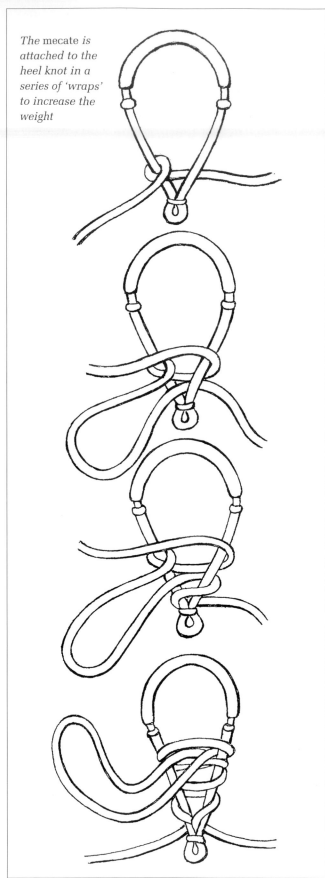

The mecate is attached to the heel knot in a series of 'wraps' to increase the weight

Also attached is a sort of throatlatch called a *fiador*, made from either mane hair or cotton; its purpose is to fix the position of the heel knot so that it does not bang up irritatingly against the lower jawbones whilst the horse is moving.

Critical to the operation is the fitting of the *mecate* to the heel knot by a system of 'wraps' which govern the extraordinarily delicate balance of the *bosal*. The nosepiece lies about 2in (5cm) above the end of the nasal cartilage with the cheeks sloping downwards to the curb groove, behind and below which lies the heel knot. Careful adjustment of the 'wraps' ensures that the weight of the rein and the heel knot act as a counter-balance to the heavy nosepiece.

At rest, or so long as the head is carried in the required position, neither the nosepiece nor the heel knot are in contact, only the side cheeks of the bosal brush lightly against the face. To correct the head position should the horse poke his nose, the hand is raised momentarily so that the nosepiece comes into contact to encourage the horse to 'tuck in', ie to bring the nose back to an acceptable position.

Should the horse attempt to evade by throwing up the head beyond the limits decreed by the adjustment, the nosepiece once more comes into contact to re-establish the head carriage. At the same time the heel knot, operating between and against the jawbones, acts in opposition to discourage any attempted evasion of the nose pressure, and also to prevent the horse from overbending and tucking the head into the chest. In skilled hands a finely adjusted *bosal* then becomes an instrument of remarkable precision.

To turn the horse, the rein, held at first in both hands, is carried outwards in the direction in which the horse is required to go, supported by the outside rein being laid against the neck. Always, of course, the action is accompanied by the appropriate shift in the rider's weight. As schooling progresses the rein is used in one hand.

The trained hackamore horse with a skilled rider executes sliding stops, pivots (the Western equivalent of the dressage pirouette but with a certain difference) as well as turns and rein-backs in a state of constant balance and at high speed. Moreover it does so

on a looped rein and, of course, without pressure on the mouth.

The apotheosis of the Western art is in the transition to the long-cheeked, often high-ported curb bit that is almost as potentially severe as those employed in the Middle Ages. The transition is made via a succession of lighter *bosals*, through a two-rein lightweight *bosal* used with two thin rope reins, until the horse can be ridden on the bit (with gossamer lightness) with just a very thin, very light *bosal* as a back-up.

Finally, the finished horse performs on the bit alone, with no noseband, and on a floating rein that exerts no more than minimal pressure. The ideal is for the horse to be ridden on the weight of a ¼in (6mm) rawhide rein, possibly given a little more body by being weighted with small, decorative pieces of metal – and that, in essence, is not too far removed from the classical ideal.

Western bits suffer as much from a mistaken nomen-clature as those of Europe, but whilst the snaffle is not unknown, they are essentially curb bits with a variety of ported mouths, or, in the instance of 'training' bits, jointed ones, and sport numerous cheek patterns.

The most fearsome is the spade bit. Its port (ie 'spade' or 'spoon') is very high and easily presses up against the roof of the mouth to remind the horse of its presence and to ensure a swift response. Like many of the American curbs the port is fitted with a roller or 'cricket' to encourage salivation and thus relaxation in the jaw.

The walking or saddlebred bits, used with bradoons, are notable for their extra-long cheeks, as are those single curbs used on the Fox Trotters and the Tennessee Walkers. The gaited breeds do not perform on the loose rein of the cow-pony, but whilst the contact with the mouth is firm, the brilliant if artificial action of these horses depends upon the bridle being used with great sensitivity.

Walking and Saddlebred bits employ a light, ported mouthpiece and are notable for the length of the cheek. The brilliant action of the horse depends to a degree on the bridle being used with great sensitivity

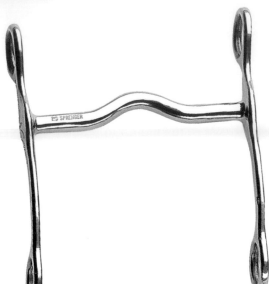

Left: An American 'cutting' bit. In effect it is a plain curb bit, used with or without a curb-strap or chain

Below: A 'black' cutting bit, a variation without too much relevance

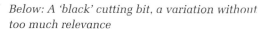

Above: Another pattern of 'cutting' bit with the cheek inclined to the rear in an effort, one supposes, to reduce leverage

Right: A 'Grazing' bit which has loops for a bradoon rein. Whether it has anything to do with grazing is problematical

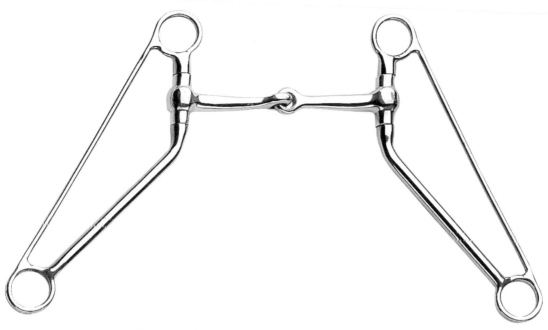

Above: Possibly the most ineptly named bit ever. It is called a 'Long Shank Snaffle'. In fact it is a curb with a fanciful cheek, but well constructed

This bit is named the 'Linda Tellington-Jones Bit', but it has been about in one form or another long before the world was blessed with Linda Tellington-Jones. It has, however, one or two interesting features

A Quarter Horse bit with a roller set lower than that in Linda's bit (left). Its presence obviates the need for a port and one imagines the bit would be as suitable, or unsuitable, for horses other than those of the Quarter Horse breed

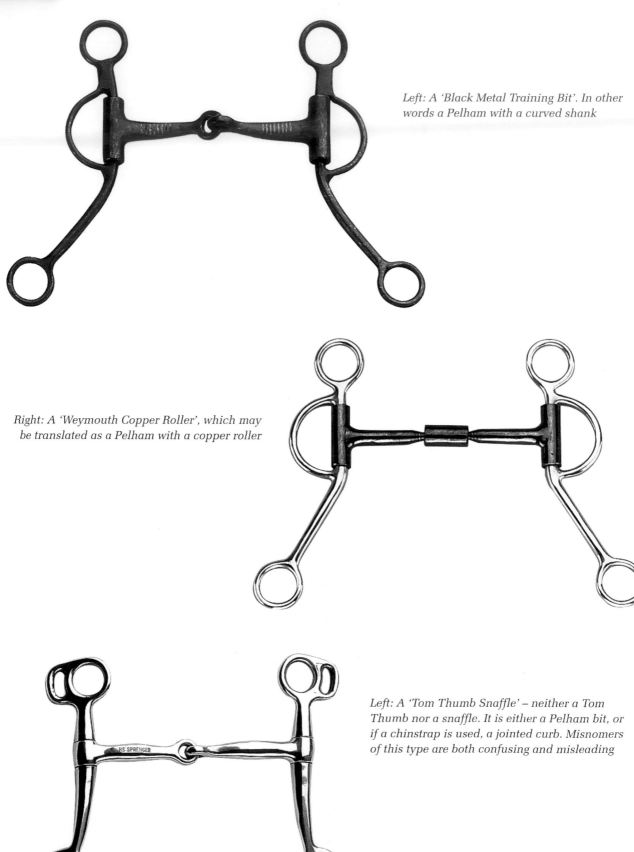

Left: A 'Black Metal Training Bit'. In other words a Pelham with a curved shank

Right: A 'Weymouth Copper Roller', which may be translated as a Pelham with a copper roller

Left: A 'Tom Thumb Snaffle' – neither a Tom Thumb nor a snaffle. It is either a Pelham bit, or if a chinstrap is used, a jointed curb. Misnomers of this type are both confusing and misleading

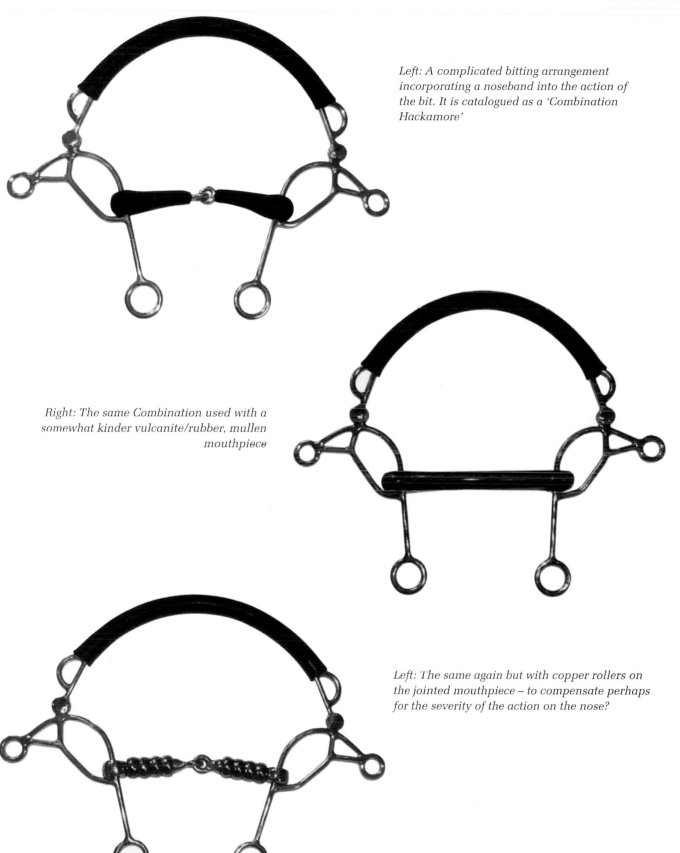

Left: A complicated bitting arrangement incorporating a noseband into the action of the bit. It is catalogued as a 'Combination Hackamore'

Right: The same Combination used with a somewhat kinder vulcanite/rubber, mullen mouthpiece

Left: The same again but with copper rollers on the jointed mouthpiece – to compensate perhaps for the severity of the action on the nose?

A bitless nose-bridle capable of powerful restraint

An equally strong bridle with a heavy, braided nosepiece

This is termed a 'hackamore', despite the ported mouthpiece. It is undoubtedly a powerful control instrument

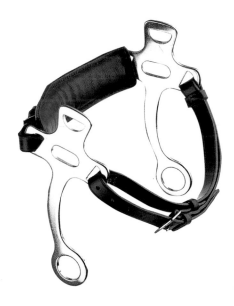

A simple nose bridle by any standards

The usual form of curbstrap

Part IV

THE MOUTH AND FITTING

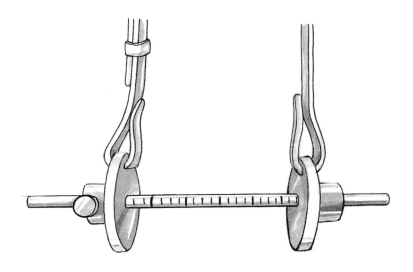

THE MOUTH AND FITTING

In recent years the equestrian world has developed an 'awareness' of the saddle as a vitally important part of the rider's equipment. We now appreciate, for instance, the need for the 'female-friendly' saddle that makes allowance for the female conformation. More importantly we recognise the influence of the saddle in relation to the horse's freedom of movement and the quality of action, and we have begun to appreciate the effect that a saddle can have on his temperament and behavioural patterns. In short, there is an 'awareness' of the saddle as a precision instrument that is directly concerned with the performance level of both horse and rider.

The 'saddle doctor', alongside the spin doctor of politics, is an established phenomenon of the last years of the twentieth century, and august bodies like Britain's Society of Master Saddlers hold saddle-fitting courses, awarding certificates to students who pass the demanding practical and written examinations. Logically, one would expect there to be a similar awareness of the bit and the fitting of the bridle, both of which are equally critical to movement, temperament and performance potential; but whilst bits exercise a considerable fascination for the riding public it is doubtful whether there is much real understanding of the theory and practice of bit selection and fitting.

It is true that the governing bodies of dressage and horse trials have regulations governing types of bit permissible in competition, but whether these are formulated from any comprehensive understanding of the subject is, I think, questionable. Furthermore the examinations for teaching qualifications include no more than a cursory study of the subject — but then neither does the curriculum require students to know about saddle construction and fitting beyond an elementary level.

On the whole, one is tempted to think that horse owners are as much influenced by current fashion when purchasing a bit as by anything else. Some will buy on the recommendation of instructors who base their advice on personal experience; others will rely on the saddlery shop salesman, who may, indeed, have specialist knowledge but is just as likely to be no better informed than the customer.

Only rarely, I believe, is a bit selected that takes into account the formation of the individual mouth. Of course, for a bit to be chosen on that basis it is first necessary to examine the horse's mouth and to understand the significance of what one finds there.

THE ANATOMY OF THE MOUTH

Whilst all the manuals instruct us to pick out the horse's feet twice daily, I have yet to find one that suggests inspecting the mouth on a regular basis. It is probably unnecessary to examine the mouth twice each day but it should certainly be looked at once a week, or even more if the horse is engaged in pursuits like hunting or jumping. Indeed, inspection of the mouth after a day's hunting or, perhaps, a cross-country event can be a very salutary experience. It may very well reveal bruising or damage caused by chafing, and that is just as reprehensible as whip marks on the quarters or flanks and no more acceptable.

However, in order to examine the mouth it is first necessary to open it and nine horses out of ten, having never been taught the exercise, will resent the often heavy-handed attempts of their owners to prise open their jaws.

In fact, teaching a horse to open his mouth on request is no more difficult than getting him to pick his feet up on the word of command. The words used

are unimportant so long as they are always the same, and delivered in the same tone of voice – one may, for instance, try saying 'Say aah', though you might just as well say 'Shut your mouth' since the horse does not understand the words – but he quickly recognises the sound and tone.

Initially it is helpful to encourage him to open his mouth by the tactful use of the fingers. As the command is given the first finger and thumb are placed round the lower jaw and inserted *very gently* into the mouth so as to lie over the bars. So long as the fingers are used gently the horse will almost certainly oblige, whereas a vice-like grip with the spare hand held firmly over the nostrils will result in quite the opposite reaction.

Once the mouth is open, the tongue can be taken out to the side, again very gently. With the tongue held in that way the horse cannot bite, even were such an ignoble thought to enter his head. But should he become alarmed and attempt to pull away, *let go* at once, otherwise you might do serious damage.

If there is any uncertainty about handling the horse in this way it would be better to invest in a Swales veterinary gag, a simple, easily managed device which keeps the mouth open and allows it to be inspected at leisure.

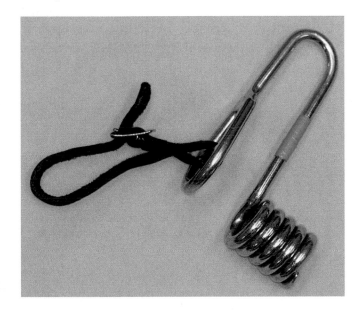

Swales veterinary gag, a simple device which keeps the mouth open for inspection. The strap fastens to the headcollar and then the gag placed in the mouth

It should be possible to get the horse to 'open up' on request within a week if the exercise is carried out twice a day or so.

With the mouth open, the *teeth*, *bars*, and *tongue* are immediately apparent and on further examination you will be able to see the formation of the *tongue channel* and the *roof of the mouth.*.

TEETH

The horse is said to have a 'full mouth' – ie a complete set of permanent teeth – when it reaches maturity at the age of about six years. There are then twelve molar teeth and six incisor teeth in each jaw, the two being separated by an area of gum known as the *bars of the mouth*.

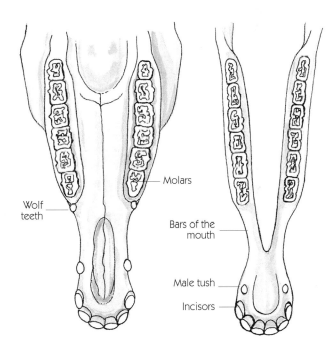

The upper (left) and lower (right) jaws of the horse

The male horse grows an additional 'tush' behind the incisors. There is no evidence of there ever having been a 'sabre-toothed' horse and the modern tush certainly serves no useful purpose. Nor, of course, are occasional *wolf teeth*, appearing just in front of the molars of the upper jaw, of any more use to the animal, although unlike the harmless tush they can cause serious trouble.

117

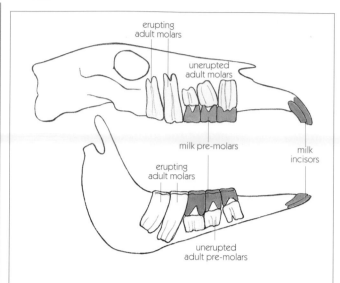

State of the teeth in the 2 year-old mouth

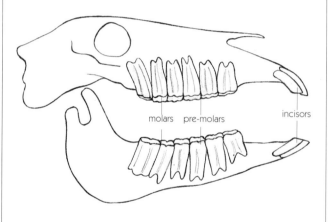

Subsequent development at 6 years

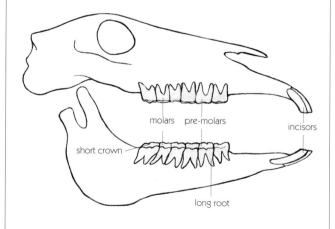

The condition at 20 years

In the first instance they are uncomfortable, and they may become painful. Secondly, the discomfort experienced will be exacerbated by the bit, and the horse will display resentment by a notable unsteadiness in the mouth and the head itself. Wolf teeth are therefore best removed as soon as they become evident. The operation presents little difficulty to a veterinary surgeon, but the condition has first to be recognised by the owner, and that will only be accomplished by regular inspection of the mouth.

There is then a particular difference in the shape of the jaws and the inclination of the teeth, and this has important consequences for the bitting arrangement. The upper jaw is always larger than the lower one, the molars of the former growing *downwards* and *outwards* while those of the lower jaw grow *upwards* and *inwards*. As a result, the enamel on the top molars and on the inside of the lower ones is not subjected to the same degree of wear as the rest of the tooth, and so the edges of the teeth can become sharp, causing pain and making it difficult for the horse to masticate his food.

For these reasons it is essential for the teeth to be regularly checked by the owner, and to receive veterinary attention at least once, and preferably twice, a year. The vet will rasp the sharp teeth smooth and will check for teeth that have become split or decayed. Older horses are more susceptible to teeth problems than younger animals and regular inspections by the owner, and probably by the vet as well, are more than ever necessary. Sharp teeth can cause laceration of the cheek or tongue and considerable pain to boot, and decayed or split teeth will have the same effect.

Teeth in this condition prevent proper food mastication and cause all sorts of riding problems. Indeed, the condition may sour the horse, particularly the more sensitive, driving him into making uncharacteristic resistances. All too often owners are unaware of what is going on in the mouth, and are tempted to change the bit or to employ some piece of extraneous equipment. It will, of course, be an unproductive exercise as well as an expensive one, and matters will only get worse, not better.

Inevitably, young horses in the process of growing

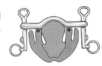

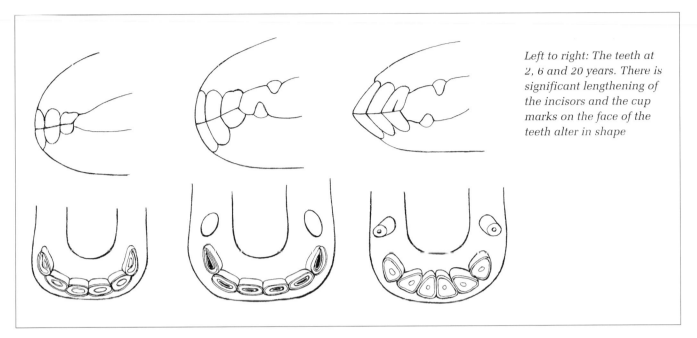

Left to right: The teeth at 2, 6 and 20 years. There is significant lengthening of the incisors and the cup marks on the face of the teeth alter in shape

up will have the occasional teething problem as the milk teeth are replaced by the permanent ones. The process is often accompanied by irritability caused by the temporarily inflamed gums, as with the human child. When the mouth is in this condition, particularly when the permanent teeth are erupting, it is advisable not to work the youngster for a day or two so that the discomfort is not aggravated by the presence of the bit. In any event a horse with toothache is unlikely to be receptive to its rider.

The gums can be eased by the application of a little tincture of myrrh or oil of cloves, but, of course, the solution depends upon the owner being aware of the problem and that, in turn, highlights the need for regular inspection.

BARS

The bars of the mouth are critical to the effective and comfortable bitting of the horse. They vary in shape between the narrow, sharp ridges of bone, thinly covered with flesh, which can be found in the young Thoroughbred type of horse, to the much flatter, heavily fleshed bars which are found in some less highly bred animals. Such bars are often accompanied by a short, thick jaw formation, whilst that of the Thoroughbred will be noticeably longer and narrower. These are important considerations in selecting a suitable bit.

Sharp, narrow bars are *exceedingly sensitive* and are easily calloused by bit pressure, particularly when applied by inexpert hands. In the process the horse is likely to become 'hard-mouthed' and can develop into a hard-pulling tearaway. Indeed, it is possible for the bar to be cut so that food can become lodged in the cavity and cause infection. Even worse, heavy hands, allied to severe bits, are quite able to splinter the bone of the bars – an unpleasant thought but not, alas, unknown. The flatter, fleshier bar by no means predisposes its owner to developing a hard mouth, but it *is* less sensitive and becomes increasingly so if it becomes calloused by the combination of an unsuitable bit and uneducated hands.

TONGUE

The tongue can also cause problems, particularly when a curb bit has to be fitted. At one end of the spectrum there is the large, fleshy tongue that seems almost too big for the mouth, at the other there is a noticeably thinner and considerably narrower organ. The fleshy tongue tends to overlap the bars and thus saves them to some extent from direct pressure, whereas the narrower one does little to protect them. Which bit, either snaffle or curb, is best suited to the mouth depends largely upon the type of bar accompanying the tongue formation.

Usually, when considering a curb bit it will be found that the fleshy tongue will take pressure so an average size port on the mouthpiece, or a shallow one, will relieve pressure on the bars. Conversely, if the bars will accept a bearing, which is preferable, the port will need to be a larger one if it is to accommodate the tongue satisfactorily.

The thin tongue, on the other hand, calls for a mild bit, perhaps a mullen mouth or an arch-mouth. A mouthpiece of soft, flexible plastic is also particularly suitable, but is *not permitted under the rules of dressage*. Why?

TONGUE GROOVE

The frequently overlooked tongue groove will also be an occasional source of problems. (One wonders whether the formulators of the dressage rules appreciate the difficulties it may cause.) Should the groove be shallow to the extent that it does not allow the tongue to lie comfortably in it, additional pressure is placed on the latter that may cause discomfort. Very often the reason why a horse puts his tongue over the bit (a habit discussed in the chapter 'Common Evasions') is to avoid the uncomfortable pressure being put on it.

ROOF OF THE MOUTH

Finally, it is worth looking at the roof of the mouth. If it is lower than the norm it may come into contact with the port of the curb bit, when the solution is to employ a mouthpiece with a shallower port. The joint of a plain snaffle may also press against a low roof, especially if the bit is too large for the mouth. The answer is to use a mouthpiece incorporating a central spatula joint, like the French bradoon.

Pressure on the roof of the mouth will result in soreness and, in consequence, to a quite understandable resistance on the part of the horse.

LIPS

Otherwise it is the lips, or rather the corners of them that can suffer from chafing. The most usual causes are:
a) too wide or too narrow a bit;
b) a bit adjusted unnecessarily high in the mouth;

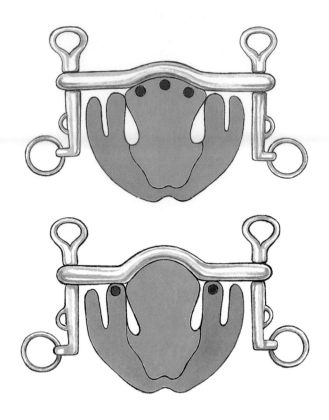

The shape of the mouthpiece governs the extent of the bearing on the bars

c) a bit hanging unevenly in the mouth because of an unequal adjustment of the cheekpieces;
d) pinching caused by wear round the hole through which the bit ring passes.

CURB GROOVE

The curb groove is the area just below the junction of the jaw branches. The area is comparatively insensitive being covered in gristle, and this is where the curb chain should lie and fit *exactly*. The fit depends upon the proper construction of the bit and the meticulous adjustment of the chain.

Above the curb groove the jaw bones are covered with only thin, sensitive skin and are therefore easily chafed. A loose adjustment of the chain in the mistaken belief that it will be less severe, ensures that it will rise up out of the curb groove to rub against the jaw bones. Bruising, and damage to the skin and bone beneath may also occur.

FITTING: GENERAL OBSERVATIONS

PARTS OF A BRIDLE

A complete bridle consists of a headpiece in which is incorporated the throatlatch (it is pronounced in the arcane British custom 'throat*lash*'); a browband or 'front'; cheekpieces or cheeks; a noseband; reins and the bit or bits.

In the double bridle there is also a sliphead, from which is suspended the bradoon; a second pair of reins; and a lipstrap. A Pelham bridle also has a lipstrap and two pairs of reins.

The sliphead is passed through the slot of the browband, the cheekpiece being fastened to the off-side ring of the bradoon with the buckle in line with that of the noseband, which lies next to the head and fastens on the near side. It is usual, and looks very much neater, if the buckles of the cheekpieces — which must, of course, be level — are in line with or just below the eye. The browband slot in a double bridle needs to be larger than that of a snaffle to accommodate the extra thickness of the sliphead.

REINS

In the double bridle, or when two reins are used with a Pelham, it is customary for the lower curb reins to be narrower by ⅛in (3mm) than the bradoon rein. Jockeys and cross-country riders usually tie a knot in the handpart of the rein at the buckle end. In the event of the rein having to be slipped to its full extent

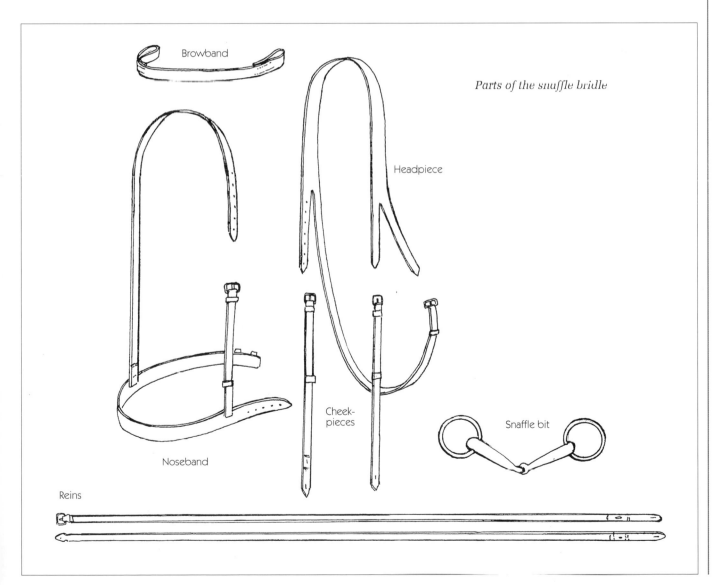

Parts of the snaffle bridle

Browband

Headpiece

Cheek-pieces

Snaffle bit

Noseband

Reins

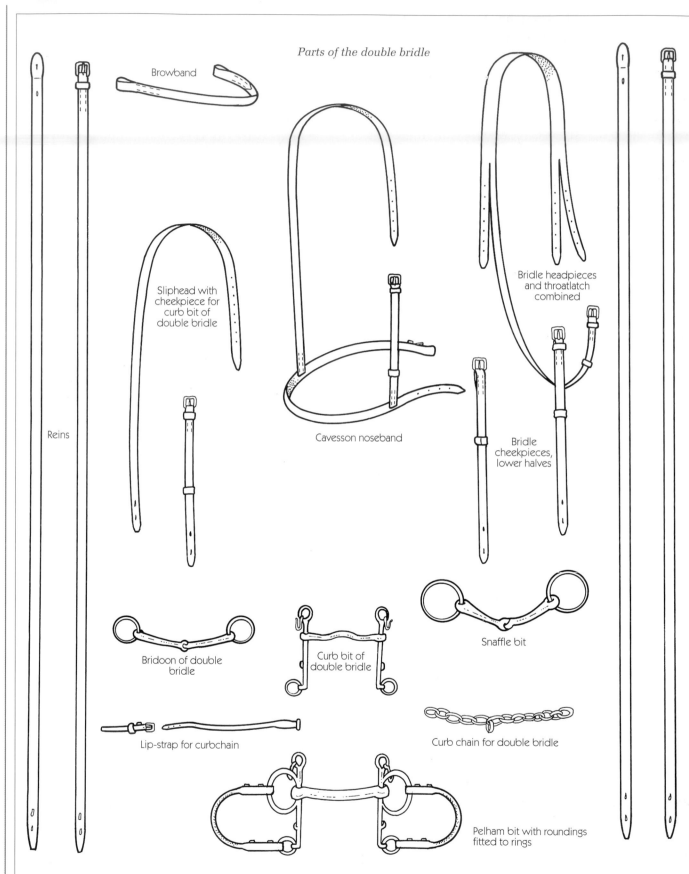

Parts of the double bridle

Browband

Sliphead with cheekpiece for curb bit of double bridle

Bridle headpieces and throatlatch combined

Reins

Cavesson noseband

Bridle cheekpieces, lower halves

Bridoon of double bridle

Curb bit of double bridle

Snaffle bit

Lip-strap for curbchain

Curb chain for double bridle

Pelham bit with roundings fitted to rings

the strain will then be taken by the knot rather than the buckle fastening, which in those circumstances might well break.

Good quality reins fasten with a buckle at the handpart. The buckle should always be on the right (off-side) rein and the point or tongue on the left, the latter lying under the right thumb – at least, that is what the manuals say, but one could be forgiven for asking 'Why? Who said so?'

In fact, the buckle in the handpart of the rein, like the cavesson noseband and its recommended fitting (see Chapter 11 'Nosebands'), has its origin in military practice and is really something of an anachronism. The buckled rein was divided so that it was possible to connect horses to their neighbours on either side, and it was in the interest of military uniformity, as well as practicality, that the buckle end was on the off-side rein and the point (or tongue) on the near-side.

ATTACHMENT TO THE BIT

Modern bridles have the bits attached by *hook studs* – perfectly safe if the studs are of European manufacture with the possible exception of studs produced or used by Eastern European countries. Buckle fastenings are safe but lacking in style; in my view loop fastenings are the best option, being both neat and unobtrusive.

Once upon a time bits were sewn into the bridle, and in those days no self-respecting hunting man would have dared appear in anything other. Mind you, there were disadvantages: the bit could not be removed when the bridle was cleaned, nor could a change of bit be effected without the expense of re-stitching and so on, which was not good for the leather.

Of necessity, times must change but I still hold that brass buckles on a bridle are for gypsies and soldiers and are otherwise an abomination..

DANGER AREAS

There are two further, critical points in fitting that relate to bits. These are to do with the *browband* and the *throatlatch*.

If the former is too short it pulls the bridle head

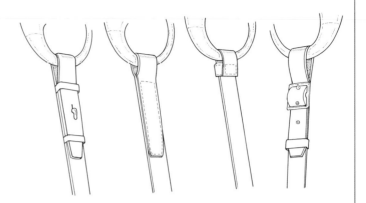

Rein fastenings (l to r): hook stud; stitched fastening; loop fastening; buckle fastening

against the back of the ears. This causes irritation which may lead to habitual head-shaking. If the browband is fitted too high it will press against the base of the ears, and this, too, will cause pronounced unsteadiness in the carriage of the head. The browband should allow for the insertion of one finger between it and the forehead, and it should be placed 1in (25mm) lower than the base of the ears.

A throatlatch adjusted too tightly will restrict the breathing and discourage flexion at the poll. Allow for the insertion of three fingers – held together and at right-angles to (not flat against) the horse – between it and the gullet.

FITTING THE SNAFFLE

A snaffle of any type should fit snugly, the butt ends of a loose ring snaffle projecting no more than ½in (13mm) on either side of the mouth. The more nearly the bit corresponds to the width of the mouth the more precise will be its action, and the danger of causing damage will be equally reduced.

Full-cheek and eggbutt patterns will always fit more closely than the loose-ring variety which, because of the construction, can pinch the lips where the ring passes through the mouthpiece.

Obviously, too narrow a bit will pinch the cheeks, but most snaffles fail because they are too wide. Such a bit will slide across the mouth concentrating the pressures on one side and probably bruising the

tongue, bars and lips on that side. If it is used with a drop noseband that prevents opening of the mouth and if, in addition, it is fitted too low, it is possible for the central joint to bear painfully on the roof of the mouth. A snaffle fitted too low may also knock up against the incisor teeth, distracting the horse and causing discomfort.

The bit is correctly fitted when the corners of the lips are just wrinkled.

Many modern snaffles are insufficiently curved on both sides of the mouthpiece to conform really well to the shape of the mouth, but it is possible to find a well curved mouthpiece which encourages an easy acceptance of the bit.

FITTING THE CURB BIT

The fitting of a curb bit is far more complex and exacting. The bradoon must certainly correspond to the width of the mouth, whilst the curb should fit as close to the outside of the lips as possible without pressing on them.

A common failing is for the bit to be too wide, when it will be displaced to one side or the other. When that happens both bar and tongue may be subjected to painful and unequal pressures, and the action of the bit will be interrupted.

Obviously, too tight a fitting will also detract from the action in a similar fashion, and again will result in discomfort and resistance.

Unequal bearing of the mouthpiece due to the fitting

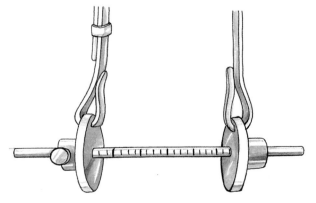

A simple mouth measure that will give an accurate width

of the bit is very soon reflected in the carriage of the head and mouth, and in turn will have an effect upon the movement which can become unlevel and irregular.

Whilst there are certain advantages to the slide-cheek curb bit, a fixed cheek will give a more accurate fit. The slide cheek, if fitted too close, makes it possible for the lips to be pinched by the movement of the cheek in the mouthpiece.

A notable failing in modern bits is that the cheek above the mouthpiece is insufficiently curved and so rubs against the face, which swells slightly above the lips, more so in some horses than in others. To allow for this conformation the cheeks should be curved away from the face. Where the cheeks are vertical in relation to the mouthpiece they can be bent outwards using a vice.

A century ago the bit was the subject of exhaustive studies by veterinarians and horsemen alike, and bitting was to all intents an exact science – although the emphasis was placed firmly on the curb bit and its introduction to the mouth. What is more, the principles laid down by those horsemen of yesteryear remain just as valid as when they were formulated.

Modern riders do some things extraordinarily well – the sports of eventing, showjumping and dressage are all prime examples and most certainly the method of riding over fences has developed in revolutionary fashion, but in comparison with their forebears they are to all intents ignorant when it comes to the practice of bitting – moreover it shows all too frequently.

If we appreciate the effect of the bit, and particularly the curb bit, then it is very clear that the positioning of the mouthpiece is of paramount importance. The optimum position is for it to be equidistant between the tush, in the case of a gelding, and the first molar teeth.

The military ruling made after the examination of hundreds or even thousands of horses, and well proven over an extended period of time, calls for the mouthpiece to be placed 'one inch (25mm) above the tush of a horse and two inches (50mm) above the corner tooth of a mare'. It is an excellent guideline, but of course, the golden rule is that the bit should be placed

Measurement of bits

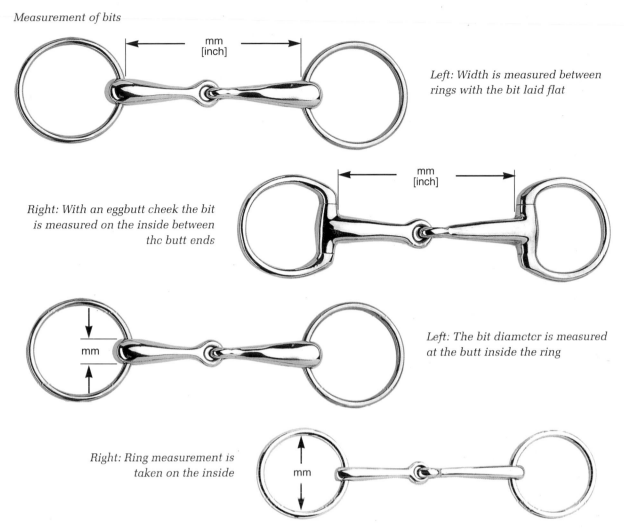

Left: Width is measured between rings with the bit laid flat

Right: With an eggbutt cheek the bit is measured on the inside between the butt ends

Left: The bit diameter is measured at the butt inside the ring

Right: Ring measurement is taken on the inside

according to the individual conformation, which may well vary a little from one animal to another.

Another very valuable guide, which also ensures that the curb chain is in the right place, is to 'place the mouthpiece on that part of the bars exactly opposite the curb groove'.

The curb chain can be adjusted by tilting the cheek of the bit so that the chain becomes operative when the cheek is inclined at an angle of 45 degrees in relation to the vertical.

If a more immediate response is wanted by those possessed of gossamer-light hands the angle can be reduced to bring the curb into action that much earlier. Such an adjustment will also result in no more than minimal poll pressure.

The curb chain is kept in place by the lipstrap, although the number of riders who see fit to dispense

with this vital item is surprising. Not only does it prevent any upward movement out of the curb groove but, according to the authorities of the last century, it will stop the cheeks from 'swinging forward and becoming reversed, as they might do, were it absent, in the event of the horse throwing up his head'. Captain M. H. Hayes (*Stable Management and Exercise and Points of the Horse*) who wrote those words, continued: 'When the cheeks are thus reversed the rider will have but little control over his mount.' I take his word for that.

Pelhams, though better suited to the horse with a short, chunky jaw structure, cause their own problems. With the exception of the Rugby Pelham with its independent bradoon ring, the longer length of the Pelham cheek above the mouthpiece will almost always draw the curb chain upwards out of the curb

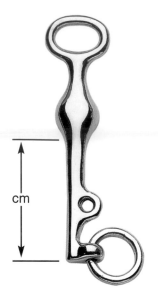

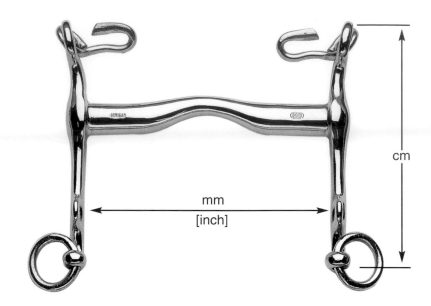

Correct method of measuring a curb bit. (Note that in this bit the eyes are inclined outward to avoid chafing the cheeks)

groove, a movement encouraged even more if the Pelham is adjusted high enough in the mouth to give snaffle action when the top rein is applied.

The bit, whilst having some advantages, is really something of a well intentioned compromise and has to be fitted as such. The best that can be done is to follow the military rule, as far as that is possible, whilst fitting the curb chain with a rubber guard. It is even more satisfactory to use a soft leather curb or an elastic one.

It is particularly important for the upper cheek parts of the Pelham to be inclined outwards and away from contact with the face.

To illustrate the meticulous attention applied to the bitting of the horse by the old horsemasters it is worth quoting Major Francis Dwyer, Major of Hussars in the Imperial Austrian Service and a noted authority of his day. In a revision of his highly regarded book *Seats and Saddles, Bits and Bitting, Draught and Harness* reprinted in 1869 he wrote of the curb bit: 'The whole art of bitting consists, so far as the mouthpiece goes, in determining how much of the pressure shall fall on the tongue and how much on the bars, and we are thus enabled, by means of an almost infinite system of graduations, to obtain exactly the degree of action required in each particular instance...'.

Later in the book Dwyer wrote, as an appropriate parting thought: '...nothing can be more certain than that the best bitting in the world is wholly useless, nay, sometimes dangerous, in bad, that is to say, heavy or rude hands'.

Part V

AIDS TO THE BIT

MARTINGALES

It is difficult to provide an exact definition of what constitutes a bitting aid. A pair of blinkers may encourage a horse to stay on the bit, in racing terms, rather than hanging behind it. A tongue strap, securing that organ, will allow the bit to act upon the mouth without the former's interference, whilst a nosenet may dissuade the tearaway from ignoring the means of control provided by the bridle. Control is, indeed, the crux of the matter, and so in the most general terms an aid to the bit can be looked upon as an item that goes some way towards preserving the action of the bit so as to provide an improved means of control and communication between rider and horse. In some instances the action is strengthened noticeably, and indeed the influence of an auxiliary to the basic bitting system, whether it be martingale or noseband, can alter the effect of the bit quite radically. In every case the purpose of an auxiliary aid is to place or even fix the head and/or the mouth so that the bit acts evenly and decisively to its full potential.

Whilst the purist may reject the use of auxiliaries, regarding them as confirmation of faults in basic training, there is no doubt that in many instances they make the rider's job easier, and achieve results without causing distress to the horse.

STANDING MARTINGALE

The simplest form of control over the head position is that provided by the **standing martingale**, an item much disparaged in modern equestrian thinking and firmly opposed in instructional practice, but one used with much finesse by the old-time nagsmen to obtain a balanced outline. Indeed, there was a time when the standing martingale was seen as an essential element in 'making the mouth', particularly when introducing

the double bridle. In competent hands, accompanied by an effective pair of legs, the standing martingale used in this context produced excellent results despite a fundamental difference in approach.

The martingale holds the head in place by exerting pressure on the nose via the cavesson noseband to which it is attached. By thus fixing the head it ensures the effective action of the bit, or bits if the double bridle is used, and allows the skilful hand to make a delicate contribution to the neck carriage and the overall outline – provided, that is, that the rider is also able to engage the horse's quarters through the medium of the driving aids: the back, seat and, of course, the legs.

Above: It is usual to adjust the martingale in line with the wither

Left: Clearly the gentleman opposite has found the proper braking system in what might appear to be a contradictory combination of noseband, standing martingale and gag

● = GENERAL AREA
  OF PRESSURE

Should the horse attempt to raise the head above the limit fixed by the martingale a correcting pressure is put on the nose

The usual fitting recommended is for the end of the martingale to be in line with the wither when, in conjunction with the noseband, the mouth will be prevented from being thrown up in an evasive action.

The restraint becomes more or less severe according to the type of noseband used. A plain cavesson,

especially if it is padded, will act as a gentle reminder that it would be appropriate to lower the head. When the nosepiece is made of rope or rolled leather the action is necessarily sharper, whilst a nosepiece inset with metal is even more powerful in its effect – possibly unacceptably so, for it can cause bruising.

The usual argument against the standing martingale is that it restricts the extension of the neck when jumping: however, this contention is entirely fallacious. When jumping, the horse's head and neck are stretched forwards and downwards (so long as the hands are following the mouth and permitting that extension). They are not thrown upwards, and if they are, then some pretty extensive re-schooling is required and perhaps an extended course of riding lessons as well.

There is no interference with extension *as long as* the martingale is fitted at the recommended length – although clearly that would not be the case if it were too tightly adjusted.

On the polo field, the standing martingale is to all intents obligatory. It is not much seen elsewhere, but if its use saves the rider getting a bloody nose as a result of a violent blow from the head of a wildly

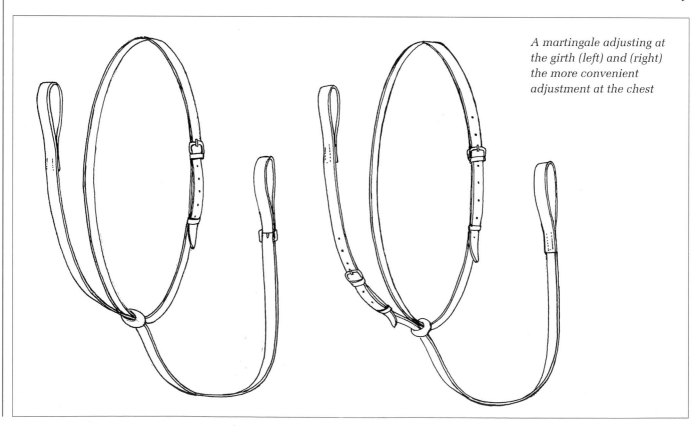

A martingale adjusting at the girth (left) and (right) the more convenient adjustment at the chest

excited horse, and if, by increasing the control, the possibility of a more serious accident is avoided, then there can be no criticism of its use. It is certainly not going to hurt the horse.

(Before World War II, the 'stick' martingale was regarded as a useful aid to 'mouthing' the horse. A stick martingale employed a rigid cane running from the breast to the rear of the noseband, taking the place of the usual leather strap. Using this device the head could be fixed with some precision, the horse being quite unable to evade the bit by throwing up the nose to come 'above' it, or by tucking the nose into the chest to become overbent and 'behind' the bit. I suspect the 'stick' martingale is now extinct – and in any event, not many modern riders are concerned with 'making a mouth' or, alas, appreciating the need to do so.)

RUNNING MARTINGALE

In far more common use is the **running martingale** which acts more directly upon the mouth than the nose. The martingale divides into two branches at the breast, each end culminating in a ring through which each rein is passed. Like the standing martingale, the

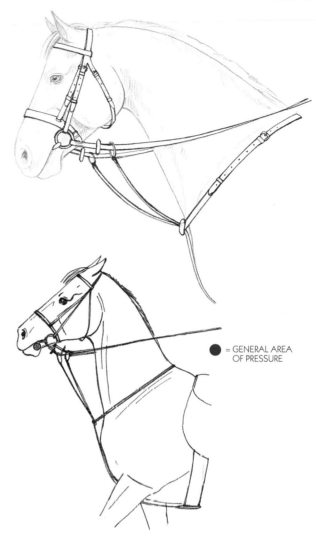

= GENERAL AREA OF PRESSURE

Above: The martingale acts on the mouth to discourage the raising of the head above the appropriate level. It is usual to adjust the martingale on a level with the wither

Left: Running martingale fitted correctly with rein stops

adjustment should be in line with the withers, so there is no angle formed between hand and mouth that would provide a point of leverage against the latter.

When the horse attempts to evade the bit by throwing up the head, the movement is corrected by the rings on the reins exerting a downward pressure through the bit across the lower jaw. This will increase the rider's control, and should the martingale be adjusted a hole or two shorter the restraining action becomes commensurately stronger, indeed closer to that of a draw rein.

131

It is very necessary for reins used with a running martingale to be fitted with 'stops' at between 6–10in (15–25cm) from the bit. Their purpose is to prevent the rings sliding forward and becoming caught up in the rein fastening or, which would be far worse, over a tooth. In the last instance the horse is likely to go swiftly into reverse and may come over backwards.

It really should not be necessary to employ a running martingale when using a double bridle. However, if a martingale is fitted it should, logically, be attached to the curb rein to support the object of lowering the head. To fit it to the bradoon rein is a contradiction in terms and action – the rein seeking to raise the head whilst the martingale acts simultaneously to bring it down.

In days when attention to detail in horse equipment was infinitely more pronounced, a martingale used on a double bridle would be fitted with a small triangular fitting that had a roller on its base so that it ran easily on the rein without the latter becoming twisted.

A further nicety in the construction of a running martingale and a very logical one for riding over a

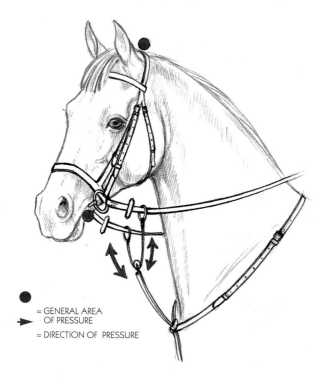

● = GENERAL AREA
OF PRESSURE
➤ = DIRECTION OF PRESSURE

The pulley martingale facilitates lateral movement and swift directional changes without putting a confusing pressure on the opposite side of the mouth. As in all martingales there is a small degree of poll pressure

jumping course is the pulley type. In this eminently sensible pattern the rings are set on a cord passing through a pulley at the top of the body strap. As a result, lateral movement and swift changes of direction can be accomplished without causing the confusing restriction on the opposite side of the mouth. In an ordinary running martingale a sharp turn to left or right puts an opposite, contradictory pressure on the other side of the mouth, a restrictive action which is avoided by the up-and-down movement made possible by the pulley fitting.

Both the standing and running martingales employ a neckstrap, a most useful aid in countering any misuse of the bit caused by a loss of security on the part of the rider. To prevent its riding up it should be secured by a rubber martingale ring fitted across the body of the martingale and the neckstrap.

VARIATIONS

The best construction of a standing martingale is for the buckle adjustment to be at the top rather than at the girth, and for the top strap to be stoutly reinforced with rawhide or something similar. This is particularly necessary for a polo martingale which has to contend with sudden and often violent upward pressures. Moreover, this construction is far easier to adjust correctly.

Two further patterns of standing martingale still to be found, usually in the American catalogues, are the **Grainger** and the **Cheshire**. The former combines the body of the martingale with a headpiece and noseband, the latter fitted in a position half-way between that of a cavesson noseband and a drop. The result is to increase the pressure on the nose, and a sliding fitment on the branches of the martingale allows an additional adjustment to make the nose pressure more or less severe. It was sometimes used in conjunction with a gag bit on very strong horses. Without doubt the horse might be made more amenable to control, but there was a risk of the device becoming unnecessarily and perhaps dangerously restrictive.

The Cheshire is another dubious piece of equipment. It is divided, like the running martingale, but

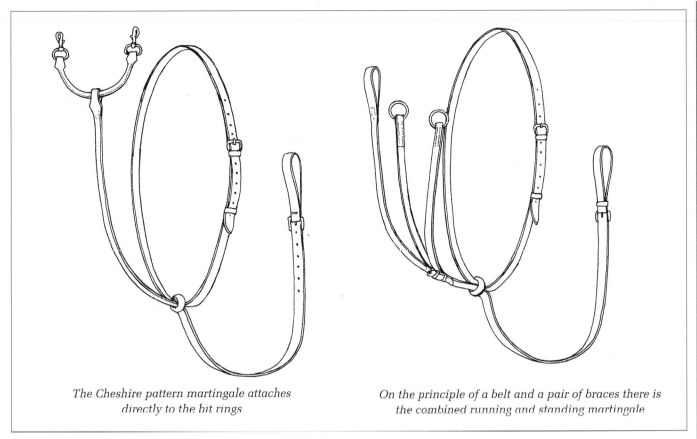

The Cheshire pattern martingale attaches directly to the bit rings

On the principle of a belt and a pair of braces there is the combined running and standing martingale

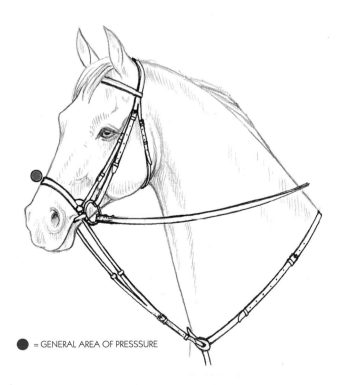

● = GENERAL AREA OF PRESSSURE

Another variation is the Grainger pattern which incorporates a noseband and can exert a fairly powerful restraint

the branches are attached by hooks directly to the bit.

Very much less Draconian in its action is the martingale which fastens to a ring on the cavesson by a stout hook incorporating a coiled spring. It allows some 'give' in the otherwise rigid martingale and is probably a helpful piece of equipment for a polo pony. (The pattern is attributed to a German source, but almost certainly it is entirely unknown in the German market.)

Other than the **pulley** martingale there is within the running martingale group the **bib**. It belongs more to the racing fraternity than to anyone else, and consists of a centrepiece of leather joining the two branches. It is a sensible precaution against an excited horse getting his nose caught up between the two branches.

Lastly there is the **Irish Martingale**, known colloquially as 'a pair of specs'; in fact it is not a martingale at all, for it exerts no influence on the bit. The purpose of this pair of Irish rings is to assist the correct direction of the rein pull and to prevent the reins being pulled over the head in the event of a fall.

133

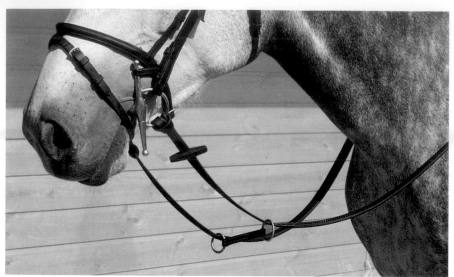

Left: The Irish martingale, known also as a 'pair of specs'. It controls the direction of the rein pull and probably prevents the reins being taken over the head in the event of a fall (note the loop fastening of the rein)

Below: A bib martingale is a useful precaution against an excited horse getting his nose between the branches of the martingale

MARKET HARBOROUGH

Finally there is that very effective, if much maligned and misunderstood, **Market Harborough**. It is sometimes catalogued (yet again) as a 'German' rein, although in Germany it is more often called the 'English' rein. It could be argued that it belongs to the family of draw and running reins, being an improved version of the basic running rein which fastens to the girth on either side of the horse and is passed through the bit rings before returning to the rider's hand (see p**146**). (The origin of the Market Harborough is obscure. In Britain it became popular in the 1950s when it was made in the West Country by a saddler named Vickery who may have first made one for a particular customer. A similar rein was used in the schooling of polo ponies in India between the wars, and a schooling rein of the same type was in general use in the civilian and military establishments of the old Austro-Hungarian Empire at the turn of the nineteenth and twentieth centuries.)

The draw rein – and perhaps the running rein too (there is a difference) – has been called 'the razor in the monkey's paw', and in that sense the Market Harborough can be regarded as something of a 'blunt-ed razor', for its action is more forgiving of the uneducated hand. In essence, it depends upon how it is viewed and used by the rider, and whether it is adjusted to act as a martingale, which function it fulfils very satisfactorily, or as a schooling rein seeking to encourage an outline.

The construction varies somewhat between one manufacturer and another, but in basic terms it comprises the usual martingale body attached to the girth between the forelegs, a neckstrap, and two branching straps which are longer and thinner than those of a running martingale. They are made from rounded leather or, more satisfactorily, from strips of rawhide, and usually culminate in small snap hooks. The branches pass through the bit rings and are then fastened to one or other of four metal dees sewn to the otherwise normal direct reins.

The arrangement allows for a considerable range of adjustment which governs accoridng to the dee-ring selected, the extent to which the head can be raised upwards before corrective action is applied. Used as a martingale, with the branches fastened to the forward dees on the rein, the action is no more complicated and no less legitimate than that of a running martingale, although it is somewhat more direct

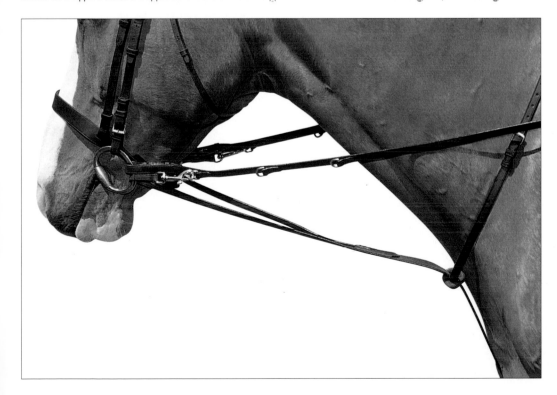

The Market Harborough belongs in reality to the group of balancing reins and is a less forceful, more sophisticated version of the running rein

135

whilst being less likely, in my view, to cause any serious discomfort.

As a means of restraint for an over-exuberant performer in the hunting field, or for that matter over a cross-country course, it is a very useful auxiliary to use, so long as the adjustment is carefully made.

Of course, if the rein were adjusted too tightly and operated by a pair of less-than-competent hands, the action could restrict the extension of head and neck, encouraging the horse to hollow his back over the fence, a matter that is neither desirable nor safe.

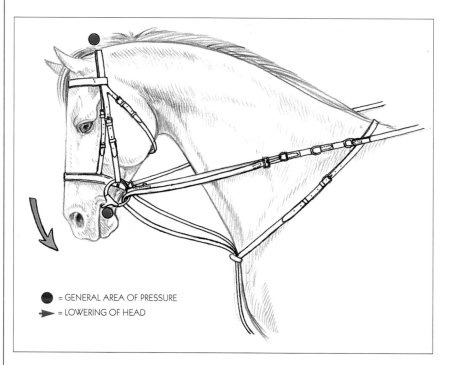

● = GENERAL AREA OF PRESSURE
➤ = LOWERING OF HEAD

The action of the Market Harborough is primarily against the mouth to bring down the nose. It is supported by a little poll pressure

As a schooling rein, the use of the Market Harborough becomes a far more sophisticated exercise and assumes some of the character of the running rein. However, because the action and the effect can be limited by adjustment, it has a less damaging potential in the hands of the less experienced rider. Used carefully it can help to place the horse in a more effective working frame, the emphasis being on the word 'carefully'.

The best method to employ is to adjust the rein

loosely at the outset and then tighten the adjustment gradually, making sure that the action never becomes over-restrictive. Thereafter the horse should be worked in the rein for just a few minutes initially, the time being progressively increased, though to no more than fifteen to twenty minutes at each schooling session.

Whilst the horse is flexed at the poll, drops the nose and relaxes the lower jaw it can be ridden normally on the direct rein; it only brings the rein into play when it abandons that position and attempts to come 'above' the bit. It is worth noting that whilst the adjustment is the responsibility of the rider, the rein is activated by the horse's own resistance to maintaining a 'correct' outline. However, with a sympathetic rider of average competence it quickly realises that submission to the rein brings immediate relief from the pressure experienced in the mouth.

Whilst the rein can materially help the rider in encouraging a working frame, and although it is less likely to be misused than a draw or running rein, so long as the adjustment is made correctly, it can, nonetheless, become both non-productive and counter-productive unless it is supported by active and effective legs. It is absolutely essential that the horse should 'advance into his mouth' and into contact with the hand as a result of the rider's driving aids pushing the horse forward from actively engaged quarters.

The danger with any sort of schooling rein acting on the head is to ignore this basic equitational truth and attempt to impose a carriage through the hand alone – ie by riding from front to back instead of vice versa. When that happens the horse shortens the neck and in consequence the stride, almost inevitably the back is stiffened, and it comes on the forehand; it will also lose any semblance of straightness, since it will seek to evade the imposed outline by swinging the quarters out and carrying them outside the track of the forefeet.

NOSEBANDS

odern thinking calls for a noseband to be used in conjunction with the bit to ensure that the latter acts effectively, and to all intents the noseband is integral to the contemporary riding scene. It was not always so, and even after it was thought fashionable or 'correct' (a word of which our predecessors made almost obsessive use) for a cavesson noseband to be worn, its purpose was largely cosmetic. It is true, of course, that it provided an anchorage for a standing martingale, but the idea of closing the mouth to ensure a more effective bit action was scarcely considered. Indeed, many skilled horsemen between the two World Wars – and there were, indeed, plenty of them – would not have countenanced the coercive closing of the mouth. It just did not enter into an equestrian philosophy which placed the emphasis on the judicious use of a curb bit to obtain the required flexions – at least, that was certainly the case in Britain. In the cavalry schools of Europe, there is evidence of increasing use of the drop noseband with the snaffle bridles used in basic training. Nonetheless, it was seen more in the light of a training aid in the progression towards the full curb bridle rather than as an aid in its own right.

Federico Caprilli (1868–1907), the Italian cavalry officer who revolutionised equestrian thinking by introducing *il sistema*, based on the rider adopting the 'forward seat' and conforming to the horse's natural outline, discarded the dominated, collected school horse, the flexions and the curb bit in favour of unfettered extension and the snaffle, but he does not seem to have ever used a noseband to keep the mouth closed.

Even as little as fifty years ago the use of a drop noseband in Britain was still a controversial issue;

today its use in one form or another is commonplace, and much of our modern riding practice depends on its presence.

CAVESSON

The most straightforward noseband is the plain **cavesson** (from the French *caveçon*, meaning 'halter') derived from the halter worn under a cavalry bridle. Adjusted as a halter – that is, allowing for the

The plain cavesson noseband taking its name from the word caveçon, *meaning halter*

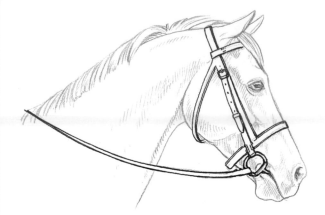

●= GENERAL AREA OF PRESSURE

X = CLOSES THE MOUTH

Above: It is possible to effect a partial closing of the mouth by lowering the noseband and fastening it snugly

insertion of two fingers between noseband and horse – it is a purely cosmetic addition to the bridle, unless a standing martingale is used. But if the adjustment is dropped down a hole or two and the nosepiece is fastened snugly, it will bring about a partial, and in some instances quite sufficient, closure of the mouth.

The most effective type of conventional cavesson (which I call, I suspect quite incorrectly, a **Grandstand**, because one was always worn by the pre-eminent cob of that name belonging to Mr Keith Luxford) allows for a very snug adjustment by having a dee set on the rear strap on the near side. The point of the rear strap can then be passed through the dee and doubled back to a

buckle sewn on the strap. Dropped down a hole or two with the nosepiece adjusted closely it will close the mouth effectively enough without its being fastened under the bit after the manner of the drop noseband – which, in itself, can become a source of resistance in some horses.

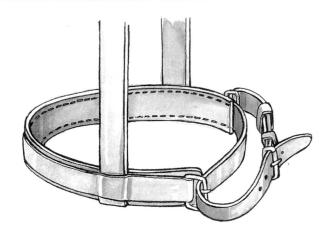

Above and below: The well designed 'Grandstand' noseband allows considerable adjustment and closes the mouth effectively with possibly less severity than the tightly fastened, lowered cavesson

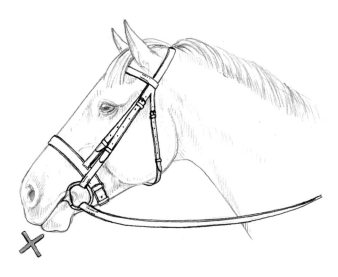

= CLOSES THE MOUTH WITH LESS SEVERITY

DROP NOSEBAND

The **drop noseband** encircles the nose and fastens beneath the bit, and closes the mouth almost completely, but it also has a further and quite complex action that alters the primary concept of the snaffle bit. As well as preventing evasion of the bit, flexion is exerted at the poll and, so far as the encircling strap allows, there will also be flexion in the lower jaw, the whole accomplished, of course, by a lowering of the head and a retraction of the nose itself. The bit itself acts very directly across the bars of the mouth to complement the lowered head position.

The action and the consequent result depend for their effect on pressure being applied to the sensitive part of the nose. It follows that if the mouth is

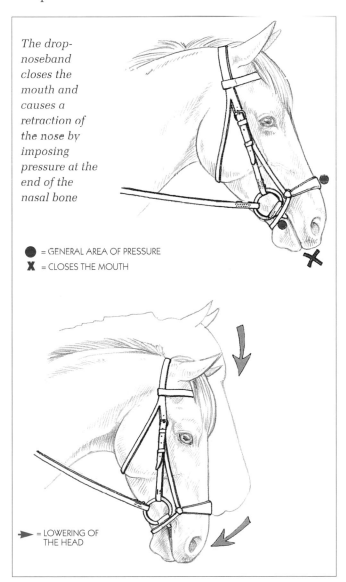

The drop-noseband closes the mouth and causes a retraction of the nose by imposing pressure at the end of the nasal bone

● = GENERAL AREA OF PRESSURE
✕ = CLOSES THE MOUTH

➤ = LOWERING OF THE HEAD

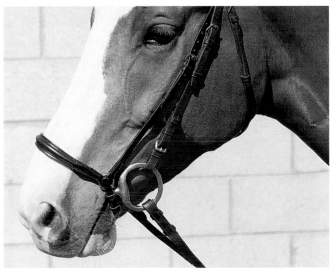

Top: The drop-noseband in action and (above) detail of the correct fitting, safely above the nostrils

139

prevented from opening, rein action is directly transmitted to the nose. In an ordinary schooling situation the nose pressure is not strong enough to cause discomfort, but when the rein is used firmly on a hard-pulling horse, control is obtained by a momentary disruption of the breathing caused by the pressure of the nosepiece. Understandably, the horse responds by dropping the nose, the bit is then able to act more decisively across the lower jaw, and the rider's control of the situation is increased in corresponding measure. (A prerequisite of control is for the nose to be held a little lower than the hand. If the horse raises the head to the point of coming 'above the bit', or if it comes 'behind the bit', over-bending and tucking its chin into the chest, the rider is quite simply out of control.)

The effect of the drop noseband is acceptable so long as the noseband is properly constructed and correctly adjusted. It becomes unacceptable when the rear strap is too short; the nosepiece will then, inevitably, be positioned too low on the face and will obstruct the nasal passages. The nosepiece should lie 2½–3in (6.5–7.5cm) above the nostrils on the end of the nasal bone; if it is adjusted lower than that the horse experiences discomfort and has difficulty in breathing easily.

A properly constructed drop will have a two-spiked ring to which headpiece and nosepiece are attached, or there will be a leather crosspiece connecting the headpiece to the nosepiece. Either method ensures that the nosepiece cannot drop downwards over the nostrils.

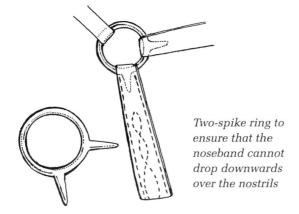

Two-spike ring to ensure that the noseband cannot drop downwards over the nostrils

FLASH

The very popular **Flash** noseband, named after a long-forgotten showjumper, was devised originally to combine the action of a drop with a noseband that would provide anchorage for a standing martingale, in days gone by an essential item in the showjumper's equipment. It is not as effective as the drop in closing the mouth but it avoids the nose pressure which is a prime characteristic of the latter. If the noseband proper is adjusted snugly it goes some way towards countering any tendency to cross the jaws.

The ubiquitous Flash noseband. The nose pressure is higher up the face

GRAKLE

The **Grakle**, named after the 1931 Grand National winner who wore one, is just as popular. Sensibly it is permissible in horse trials dressage tests but is specifically excluded in the rules of dressage, a matter that allows one to question the competence of the dressage hierarchy in respect of its pronouncements about horse equipment.

If the purpose and action of the noseband is but imperfectly understood, the proper construction is just as much at fault, and it is rare to find a properly made Grakle.

In a Grakle made to the original pattern, the pressure point on the nose is sited at the crossing of the face straps, and can be adjusted to increase or decrease the intensity of the action in a way not possible with the Flash or the conventional drop. Ideally

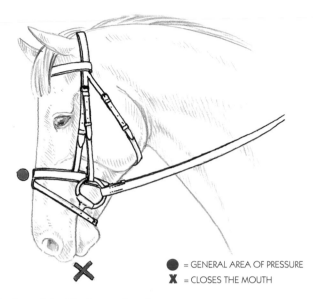

Action of the Flash noseband

● = GENERAL AREA OF PRESSURE
✗ = CLOSES THE MOUTH

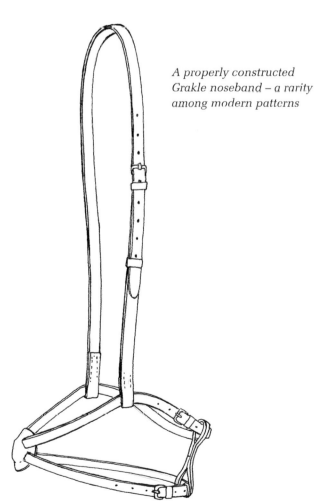

Detail of the Flash. Note that the headpiece is slotted through the noseband rather than stitched to it

A properly constructed Grakle noseband – a rarity among modern patterns

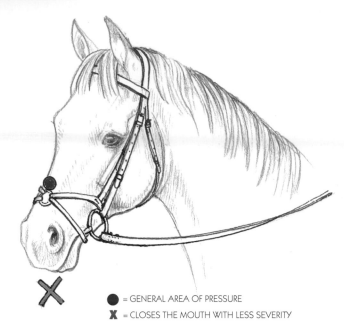

● = GENERAL AREA OF PRESSURE
✗ = CLOSES THE MOUTH WITH LESS SEVERITY

Action of the Grakle. It also discourages crossing of the horse's jaws

the straps are shaped, or curved, so that their highest point is where they join the headpiece. The top strap encircles the jaws above the bit – indeed, halfway up the face – and the lower one below it. Their position is fixed by a short connecting strap lying behind and between the jaw bones. The strap is critical to the closing of the jaws along their length and the effective prevention of any attempt to cross the jaws.

Nose pressure is less restrictive than that imposed by the conventional drop because it is localised higher up the face.

(The modern Grakle, a figure-of-eight device, rarely, if ever, includes the rear connecting strap.)

OTHER NOSEBANDS

The above are the principal nosebands of modern equitation; there are others, although today these have possibly no more than a curiosity value.

There is, for instance, the 'blunt instrument' of the noseband tribe, the **Kineton** or **Puckle**, invented by Mr Puckle who lived at Kineton. It exerts a powerful restraint through pressure on the nose but makes

no attempt to close the mouth, or to incorporate any niceties in its action.

It comprises two metal loops fitted to the inside of the bit rings and behind the mouthpiece; these are connected to the headpiece and an adjustable nosepiece reinforced with a strip of shaped metal. The Kineton may have a use in restraining the 'fallen angel' determined to take off into the blue come what may; or it may be popped on to a racehorse to ensure that it gets to the post without incident: once there, it is removed. (Quite inexplicably the Kineton was once listed as permissible in Pony Club competitions – ye Gods!)

The Kineton, something of a 'last ditch' measure

Right: A well-fitted Grakle with the nose pressure high up the face

AIDS TO THE BIT

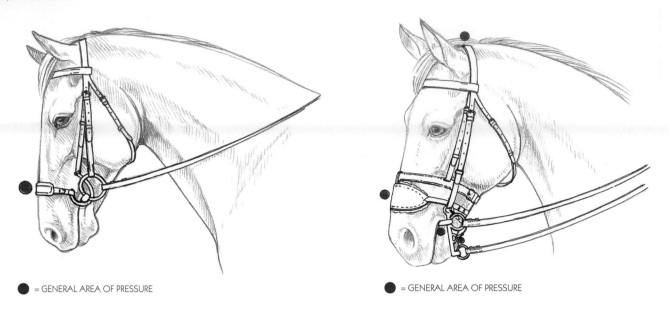

● = GENERAL AREA OF PRESSURE   ● = GENERAL AREA OF PRESSURE

Above: The Kineton is capable of exerting strong pressure on the nose

Above right and right: The Bucephalus or Jobey noseband which adds nose pressure to the action of either a double or Pelham bridle. The perfect 'gentleman's gadget'

My favourite curiosity is the **Bucephalus** or **Jobey** noseband. Bucephalus was the mount of Alexander the Great, and carried that legendary leader to the very banks of the Indus and was his partner in a thousand enterprises of note. What is quite certain is that he never wore a Bucephalus noseband. Jobey was of more humble origin and probably did.

It is a noseband for use with a double or Pelham bridle, and in former days, when polo was the game 'of English gentlemen and Indian princes', was a very useful and marvellously discreet help on the polo field.

It is no more than a swelled strap tapering at each end to a small metal dee. There is a small strap and buckle at the centre of the nosepiece to secure the device to a cavesson noseband. The ends of the

Controller noseband. It does indeed increase the rider's control but there are other more effective nosebands to achieve that end

144

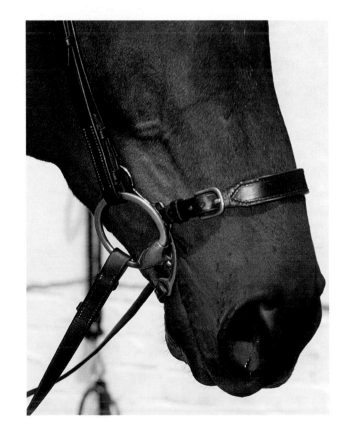

The sheepskin noseband of the racecourse is derived from the 'shadow roll' of the harness racing track. It may help concentration but has no restraining action

straps are then passed round the jaws so that the off-side dee fastens to the near-side curb hook of the bit and the near-side dee to the off-side hook. As a result there is the restraint of nose pressure added to the usual pressures of the bitting arrangement.

I used a Bucephalus with a Rugby Pelham on one or two Indian-bred polo ponies and also on an enthusiastic hunter. In all instances it worked beautifully and was the perfect 'gentleman's gadget'.

DRAW & RUNNING REINS

The patterns of draw or running reins available are very numerous, but despite one or two ingenious variations the principles underlying their use remain the same.

For the most part these reins are condemned by national governing bodies, the most usual aphorism employed being 'running reins are for experts, and experts don't use them', a statement which is patently untrue. Skilled professionals do use these reins on a temporary basis, and some of them go so far as to endorse (commercially, one supposes) a particular pattern. It is not unreasonable, therefore, to assume that some advantage is to be gained from their use, although whether the same results will be obtained by the inexperienced is improbable.

Among the equestrian governing bodies the German National Equestrian Federation is almost alone in giving a cautious, if limited, approval to the reins. It states that certain circumstances 'may justify the temporary use of running reins (mainly as a time-saving effort)', but only with horses of an 'extremely difficult conformation'. The statement begs the question, 'Why bother with a horse of an "extremely difficult conformation", and in that situation how humane is the use of the rein?'

It is legitimate enough to correct defects caused by bad schooling. Whether it is acceptable to attempt the correction of inherent physical deficiencies is more questionable. (There is also a tacit approval for the rein in teaching the *Schaukel*, the seesaw movement of backward and forward steps made without the intervention of a halt.)

THE DIFFERENCE

It is arguable as to what constitutes a draw rein and what a running rein, and whether there is a difference in their action.

The invention of the running rein is attributed to the sole English Master, William Cavendish, Duke of Newcastle (1592–1676), and it was in common use throughout the most glorious period of 'classical' equitation.

The rein 'runs' from beneath the saddle flap, or

Below: The difference between the draw rein (left) and the running rein (right)

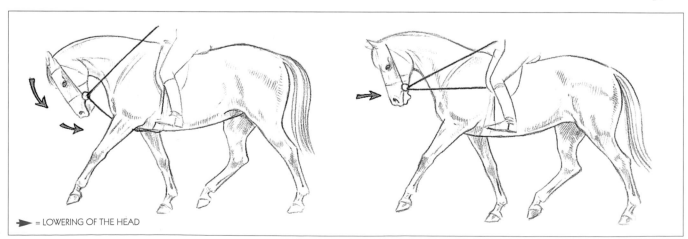

➤ = LOWERING OF THE HEAD

Left: Running rein attached under the saddle flap

Right: Draw reins attached between the forelegs and somewhat stronger in their effect

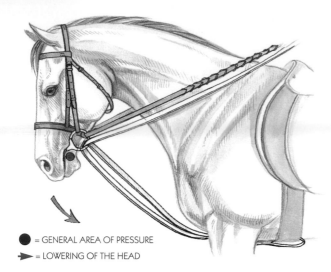

● = GENERAL AREA OF PRESSURE
➤ = LOWERING OF THE HEAD

The fitted draw rein with the riding rein attached above it. It is never advisable to use either draw or running reins without the accompaniment of the riding rein. In any event draw/running reins need to be used judiciously and it is imperative that they be supported by active legs

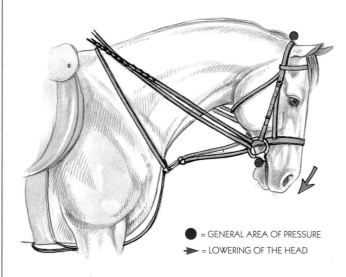

● = GENERAL AREA OF PRESSURE
➤ = LOWERING OF THE HEAD

A variation on the fitting of draw or running reins. This pattern has its fastening at the chest and probably produces a softer action as a result. There is always the possibility of some lowering pressure on the poll but in the whole context of the rein it is not especially significant

just below it, and through the bit rings before returning to the rider's hand. It is then passed from *the inside to the outside* of the bit ring, a method that reduces, if only by a little, the inward squeezing action against the face that becomes more noticeable when it is fitted in the opposite fashion.

The draw rein is similarly fitted with regard to its passing through the bit rings, but it originates at the girth and passes upward to the bit between the forelegs.

The methods of attachment are responsible for a difference in the action, the draw rein being by a little the more direct of the two since it 'draws' the head downwards as well as causing the nose to be brought inwards. The running rein does much the same, but it places less emphasis on lowering the head.

In fact, Newcastle did not differentiate specifically between the two. In the earliest depictions he uses the running rein as described, but later pictures show him using both reins, and one must conclude that he did so appreciating the difference in the action and using one method or the other as the circumstances dictated.

PURPOSE

The purpose of the reins is to assist in shortening and rounding the outline, and to counter the evasions that might frustrate that end. Most young horses when asked to work within a frame created by the rider's legs and hands, will, initially, seek to avoid the restraint. Most commonly, they swing the quarters to one side or another. Some may duck the nose or, conversely, attempt to throw the head upwards, or they may twist at the poll. The problem is overcome by the rider's legs pushing the horse into lightly restraining fingers and then, when the horse responds, to ride within the frame created for just a few strides. Little by little the number of strides made within the required frame is increased, and so it goes on. However, it takes time, though a time that can be reduced by judicious use of the rein. Even so, it is still a matter of little by little.

To be effective, the rein, or reins, need to be used in conjunction with a second rein attached directly to the bit. The schooling rein is then held 2in (5cm)

Correct, tactful use of the draw rein in conjunction with an active leg

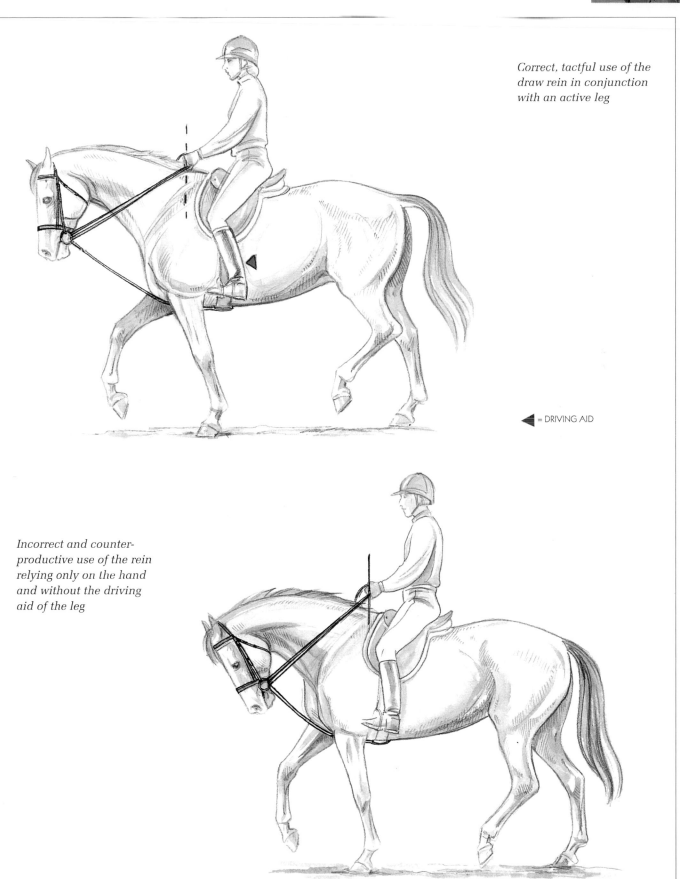

◀ = DRIVING AID

Incorrect and counter-productive use of the rein relying only on the hand and without the driving aid of the leg

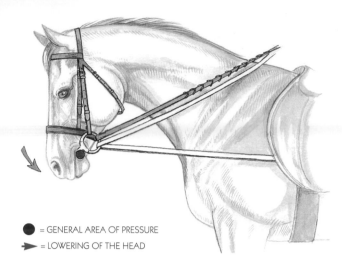

● = GENERAL AREA OF PRESSURE
➤ = LOWERING OF THE HEAD

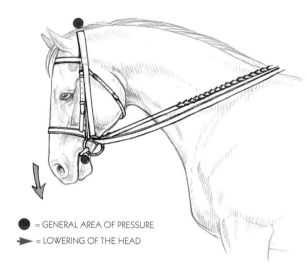

● = GENERAL AREA OF PRESSURE
➤ = LOWERING OF THE HEAD

Top: The running rein fitted to bring the nose downwards and inwards

Above: Here the rein passes over the poll, through the bit rings to return to the hand. Obviously poll pressure is increased considerably but on the whole the rein used in this way is more likely to create problems in respect of shortening the neck to the detriment of the overall shortening of the frame

shorter than the direct rein. When the driving aids push the horse forward into the bridle, the bit will act over the bars of the mouth and control is then passed to the direct rein. Should the horse seek to evade and lose the outline, the schooling rein will again be brought into use.

If the rider is tactful, the horse, which is far from being stupid, will quickly appreciate that submission to the direct rein saves him discomfort.

Constant use of the draw rein only produces constant resistance on the part of the horse, and again it is the ability of the rider to use the legs effectively that is a pre-requisite for success. The ideal is for the rein to produce a result by *suggestion* – never by force.

It is untrue that experts do not use running reins, but it is a fact that 'running reins are for experts…'. Use of the rein by riders with less than effective legs is almost always disastrous. Such riders come to rely on the rein and are deceived into thinking that they are shortening the outline when, in fact, they are only shortening the neck and not the whole horse.

Below: The Schief-Zugel rein introduced by Louis Seeger, the pupil of the Spanish Riding School luminary, Max von Weyrother. It was in common use in the nineteenth-century cavalry schools of Europe

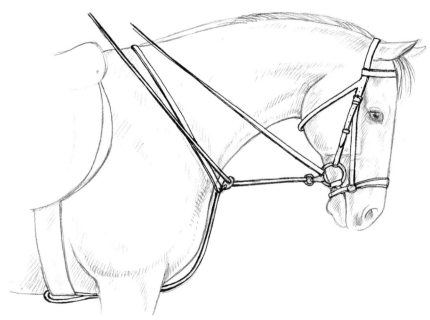

SIDE-REINS

ide-reins can be used for short periods when the horse is ridden under saddle to help the rider establish an acceptable frame within which the horse can be worked to best advantage. They are also employed as an additional measure to strengthen the control system on the polo field.

However, their principal purpose is involved in the early schooling of the horse on the lunge. In this context they act to encourage a balanced carriage and as an introduction to making contact with the bit. They do not, or should not, seek to *impose* a head carriage by being too tightly adjusted. They are fitted once the horse has become accustomed to circling the trainer on the lunge and is obedient to the verbal commands.

Initially the reins are loosely adjusted; they are then shortened gradually as the training progresses. The ideal is for the rein to loop slightly when the horse is in movement and in a satisfactory carriage. If they are any tighter than that there is the risk that the horse will attempt to evade the contact by taking the nose back and putting itself 'behind' the bit. Conversely, if the

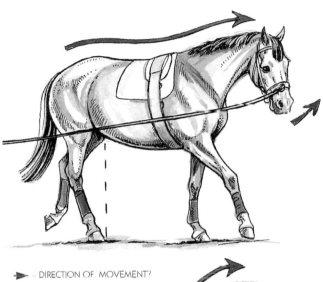

➤ = DIRECTION OF MOVEMENT?

Right: Side-reins used to encourage a balanced carriage and a shortening of the outline

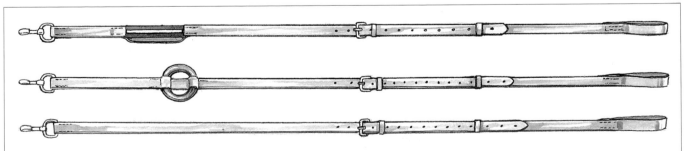

Three common patterns of side-rein. The top rein is inset with elastic, the centre rein employs a rubber ring and the third is the plain rein which many authorities claim as being more effective

rein is uncomfortably tight there is every likeli-
hood of the horse hollowing the back and raising
the head to come 'above' the bit.

The side-rein of the classical schools was,
and still is, a plain leather rein with ample
adjustment which is attached to the bit ring in
front and to a dee on the body roller behind. My
personal preference is for a roller fitted with
three dees on each side at varying heights. It is
then possible to adjust the height as necessary
and in accord with the carriage assumed by the
horse. A leather rein, or possibly one made of
stout, tubular web, is always preferable to nylon,
which is too light to give any significant weight
to the rein or the bit.

Reins inset with rubber rings or a strip of elastic to produce a 'give and take' effect may have a
certain appeal, but the theory is a fallacious one.
Indeed, such reins may give positive encouragement to evasions, the 'give' and more particularly the 'take' causing the horse to evade the
tension by coming away from contact with the bit
and tucking the nose in towards the chest.

There is a school of thought that advocates
adjusting the inside rein (the left on the circle
left and vice-versa) a hole tighter than its partner
so as to allow for the neck to be bent in the direction of the movement. It sounds logical, but is
the cause of all sorts of problems. It is likely to
encourage the horse to lean on the inside of the
bit or to retract the nose to avoid it. The bodyweight is then carried on the inside shoulder
and the quarters are pushed outwards and prevented from following the track of the forefeet.
Evenly adjusted reins, if they are not too tight,
allow quite sufficiently for the necessary bend.

*Fitting. Top – correct; centre – too tight, causing
overbending and resistance through the body;
below – too tight again, causing the horse to resist by
raising the head and hollowing the back*

BALANCING REINS

Balancing reins have an undoubted effect upon the bit. In reality they extend the principle of the basic running/draw rein and, like the latter, seek to influence the outline of the horse, placing it within an effective frame, and doing so in pretty quick time. The modern ones claim to encourage and establish a correct muscular formation, and there is no doubt that they are more comprehensive in their action than the relatively straightforward running rein.

Probably the most important of them in recent years is the rein developed, perfected and aggressively marketed by the late Peter Abbot-Davies, and its origins can be traced to long before the running reins of the classic Renaissance period. Something very like it existed in the horse-lore of the pre-Christian era as part of chariot horse harness and operated as a sort of 'tail rein'. Incontrovertible evidence of its existence is provided on the façade of the Temple of Rameses III at Medinet Habu, and that relief is dated as belonging to the twelfth century BC.

Between the wars, balancing reins – or bending or mouthing tackles as they were sometimes known – were part of the equipment of many professional yards producing horses and ponies for sale. Blackwell's dumb-jockey was a very popular pattern and was still advertised in American catalogues of the mid-1950s. Essentially, it was an improvement on existing and earlier patterns that were certainly employed as training aids during the period of 'classical' equitation.

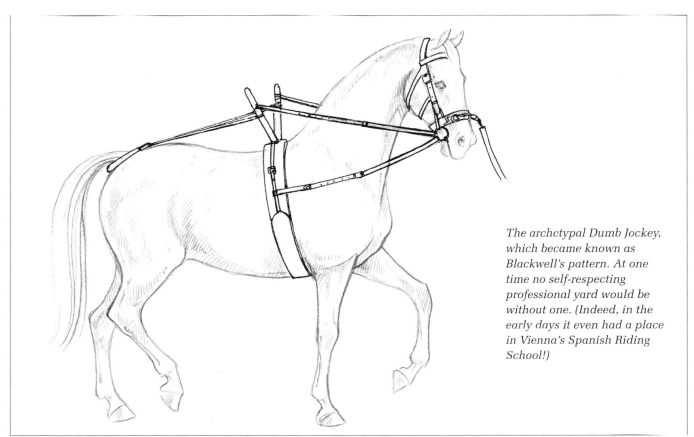

The archetypal Dumb Jockey, which became known as Blackwell's pattern. At one time no self-respecting professional yard would be without one. (Indeed, in the early days it even had a place in Vienna's Spanish Riding School!)

153

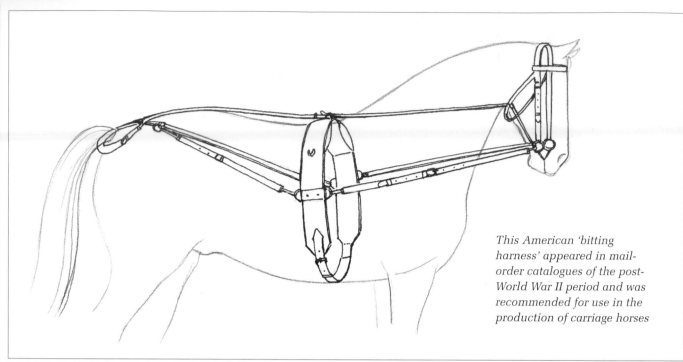

This American 'bitting harness' appeared in mail-order catalogues of the post-World War II period and was recommended for use in the production of carriage horses

Pictorial evidence shows that such equipment was in regular use at the Spanish Riding School in Vienna during the seventeenth century.

THE DUMB-JOCKEY

In the period prior to World War II, despite the prevalence of dumb-jockeys and the schooling philosophy to which they belong, the dumb-jockey itself was regarded as a highly controversial piece of equipment. The establishment inveighed mightily against it, as it was to do in more recent times against contemporary patterns of balancing harness. It was argued that the dumb-jockey produced a stiff, hollow outline; that it was unduly restrictive; and that it detracted from free forward movement. Some authorities, indeed, condemned it as being cruel. Without doubt there was a potential for great cruelty, and in some instances its use on carriage horses, an area in which it was extensively employed, might well have amounted to unacceptable abuse.

Of course it does not find favour today, when our philosophy in the early training of the horse is concerned with the long, low outline (almost, on occasions, to the detriment of a more advanced shape).

Nonetheless, the dumb-jockey along with the outline it produced, and which Caprilli had rejected outright in the formulation of his forward system of riding, exactly reflected the thinking of European horsemen, and perhaps, to an extent, that of the classical schools also, well up to the early years of the twentieth century.

THE DISTAS TACKLE

A later variation, more complex and more sophisticated, was the **Distas** bending tackle which to my certain knowledge was being made and sold as late as 1965. It is very doubtful if it could be obtained today, even if it were wanted, but for the serious horseman and woman it is worth studying on account of its great ingenuity and the purpose that lay behind its design. Furthermore, it emphasises once more the old principles involving the use of the tail to produce an outline and a made mouth.

The bridle is frankly elaborate but employs the simple four-ring Wilson snaffle to put pressure on the nose rather than the mouth. The nosepiece, held in place by the face strap, is made of elastic. Pulleys are fitted each side of the headpiece. The bridle is

completed with a 'Jodhpor' polo curb, an item still in production today, and a cord overcheck after the harness horse pattern. (The Jodhpor curb lies between the jaw-bones.) The rest of the tackle consists of a roller with an elasticated backstrap, a dock crupper and a pair of extended side-reins.

The overcheck passes from the curb rein through the bit to the pulleys at the bridlehead and then through the smaller ring set on the elastic of the backstrap, where the adjustment – a very crucial one – is made by a simple bow knot. The curb is kept in place with a lipstrap

and the crupper adjusted so that it just raises the tail.

The effect of the side-reins is to bring in the head to a near-vertical plane as the result of nose pressure – not that of the bit – whilst the curb and overcheck raise the head and prevent evasion by overbending.

It was claimed that when correctly fitted, the tackle operated the whole horse, the loins being brought into play and the horse flexed at the poll and not in the lower third of the neck (a common fault in present-day schooling.) Initially it was recommended that it be left on for just a few minutes at a time; thereafter, the

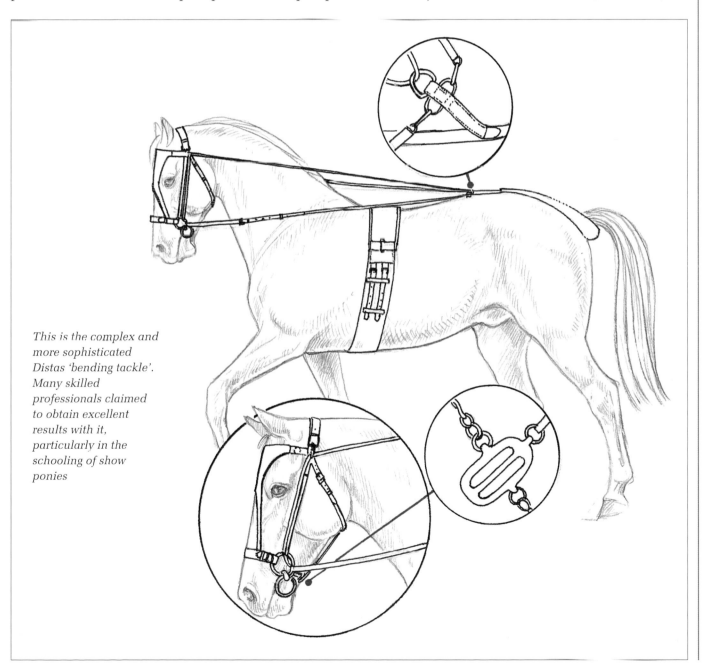

This is the complex and more sophisticated Distas 'bending tackle'. Many skilled professionals claimed to obtain excellent results with it, particularly in the schooling of show ponies

greatest benefit accrued from working the horse loose in it, for short regular periods. With the tackle fitted, it was then possible to drive the horse in long-reins.

I believe the experts obtained remarkable results with this tackle, but there is no denying that it required the most painstaking adjustment and great experience when working the horse.

Both these reins recognised the need to involve the quarters of the horse, the Distas more than the dumb-jockey. During the period there were also simplified mouthing tackles, like the Carlburg, which was probably devised in Leicestershire dealing yards. Most of them, however, operated only on the horse's forehand and failed on that account, as do many of the modern 'short-cut' reins.

Obviously, some of these reins in skilled hands must have produced satisfactory results, even though they are at variance with the principles we hold today. Their passing from the equestrian scene marks, perhaps, another watershed in the long progression of horse training.

The Abbot-Davies rein encouraged the production of other, similar reins, very few, if any of which approached the potential of the original. All too often it is the less-than-competent who are attracted to balancing reins and use them as a means of short-cutting the quiet, logical progression of basic schooling. In those circumstances it is possible for the horse to become stiffened throughout the body, for the paces to become impossibly restricted and for the horse, with good reason, to be made sour and resentful.

THE ABBOT-DAVIES REIN

In all this welter of artificial devices the Abbot-Davies rein stands on its own, and it should be recognised as belonging to a different category altogether. Unlike its predecessors it is designed primarily for use under saddle and thus incorporates a high degree of rider involvement.

It also epitomises in its introductory action the practice of 'tail-reining' which has been with us in one form or another ever since Rameses and probably before. Nonetheless, it contrives to avoid the pitfalls of the dumb-jockey type of balancing rein, by being conceived as a training system in its own right. Clearly it can be used correctively, but it is far from being a last-ditch instrument of coercion.

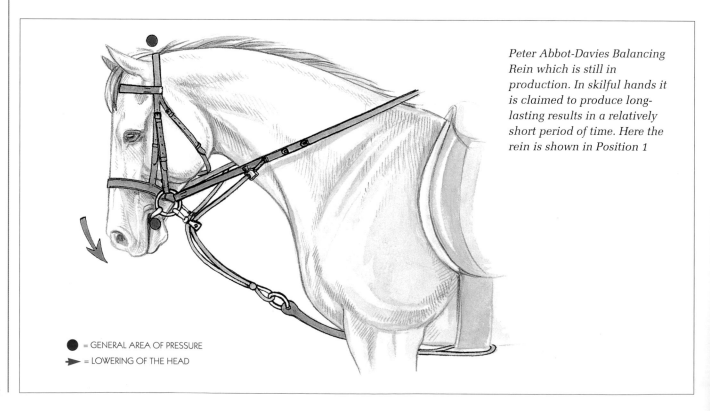

Peter Abbot-Davies Balancing Rein which is still in production. In skilful hands it is claimed to produce long-lasting results in a relatively short period of time. Here the rein is shown in Position 1

● = GENERAL AREA OF PRESSURE

➤ = LOWERING OF THE HEAD

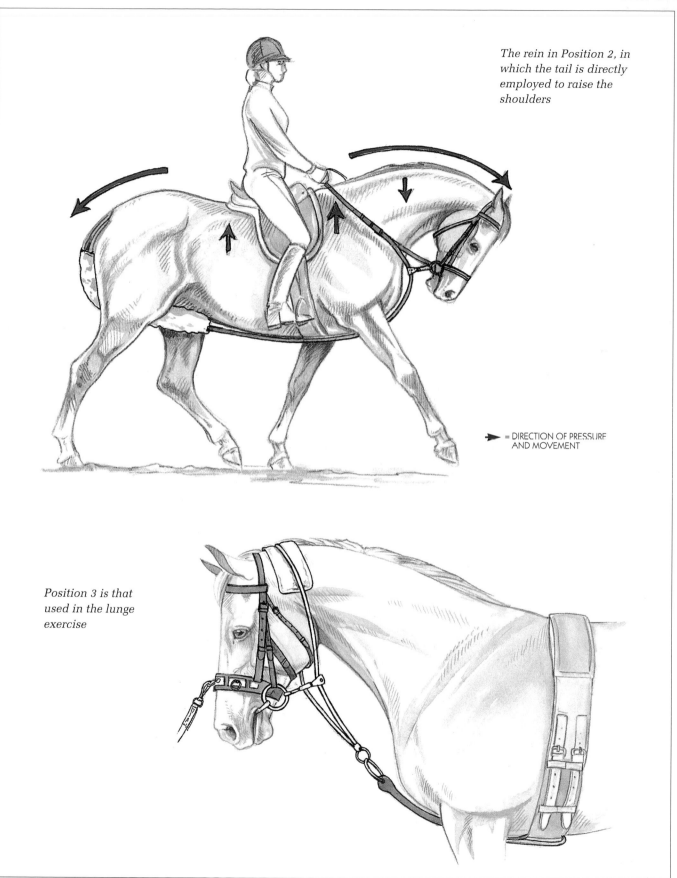

The rein in Position 2, in which the tail is directly employed to raise the shoulders

➤ = DIRECTION OF PRESSURE AND MOVEMENT

Position 3 is that used in the lunge exercise

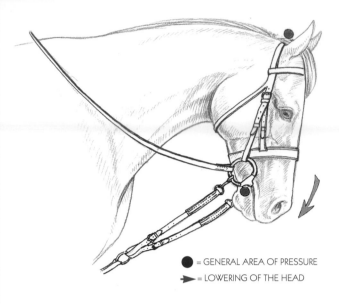

● = GENERAL AREA OF PRESSURE
➤ = LOWERING OF THE HEAD

Above and below: This is the Harbridge rein, a simplified 'balance' rein which, in essence, is no more than the old Cheshire martingale

Even so, and despite its built-in safeguards to prevent resistance, it is a tool that remains only as good as the man or woman who operates it, a truism that can be applied to any equitational aid from the snaffle upwards. For that reason the late Peter Abbot-Davies marketed the device from a specialist riding centre in Northampton devoted to its use and prepared to instruct intending purchasers.

Foremost among the balance-type reins is the old straightforward running rein. In essence Abbot-Davies combined the principles of tail-reining with those of the running rein, mitigating the potentially inhibiting action of the latter by the use of a 'shock-absorbing' system depending upon an ingenious pulley and a precision-built spring arrangement.

Horsemen have always been aware of the tail as a solution to some of their equestrian problems. Hold up the tail of a fractious foal and it almost immediately comes to hand; moreover with the tail held up it is quite unable to kick. To teach a horse to run out in hand without hanging back it is only necessary to put a cord round the dock and bring the ends of the rope forward to pass through the bit rings: holding the rope ends, one then moves off and the horse follows willy-nilly. It is, indeed, being led from its tail, and the same strategem can be used on a reluctant loader. (With a little ingenuity a tail-rein can also be used to advantage on the ridden horse, although I imagine its use was confined to the more recalcitrant subject, who jibbed and/or bucked with some determination.)

To achieve the object of creating an effective outline the Abbot-Davies rein was concerned to build up the muscles of the neck and back correctly and in a relatively short space of time – or, of course, it could be used to correct a faulty muscle structure. As a result of schooling with the rein the shoulder is raised, the back is rounded and the quarters are fully engaged under the body, the horse moving with head and neck lowered and the former strongly flexed.

There are three positions for operating the rein:

1 Attached from mouth to girth by means of a rubber rod via the 'shock-absorber' pulley and spring.

2 From mouth to tail with a rope that is passed through a soft sheepskin sleeve, again via the shock-absorber.

3 From mouth to behind the ears by means of a rubber connection.

The last position is usually associated with lunge work, but it can also be used under saddle. It produces an exaggerated lowering of the head and neck causing the shoulders to rise and encouraging greater engagement of the quarters.

The second position is critical to the system and acts to introduce the horse to the rein and to produce the initial rounded outline. However, it needs to be employed sparingly and with sympathy: used for too long a period by the inexperienced it can become an abuse of the horse, causing pain and resentment. Two short lessons of no more than fifteen minutes when the training begins are enough to place the horse in the rounded outline. Thereafter the rein should take on a booster role, being used for just a short period once a month, simply to re-establish the frame.

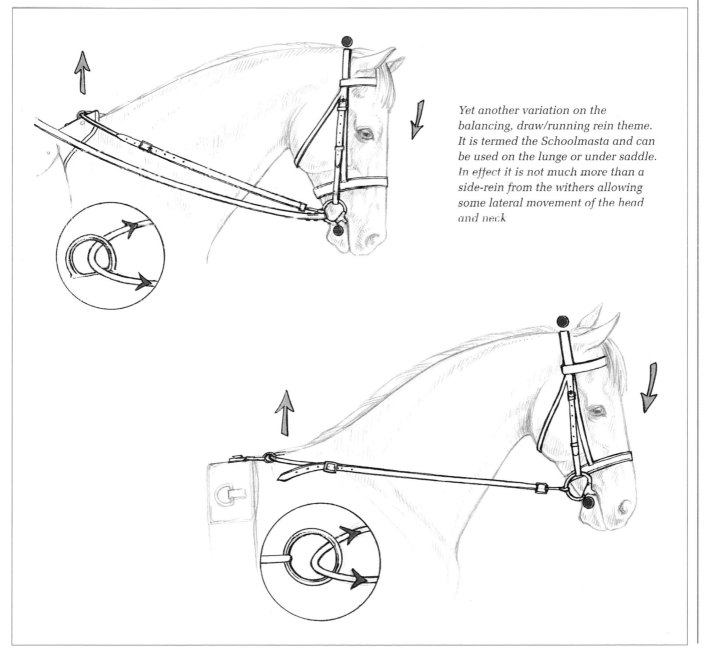

Yet another variation on the balancing, draw/running rein theme. It is termed the Schoolmasta and can be used on the lunge or under saddle. In effect it is not much more than a side-rein from the withers allowing some lateral movement of the head and neck

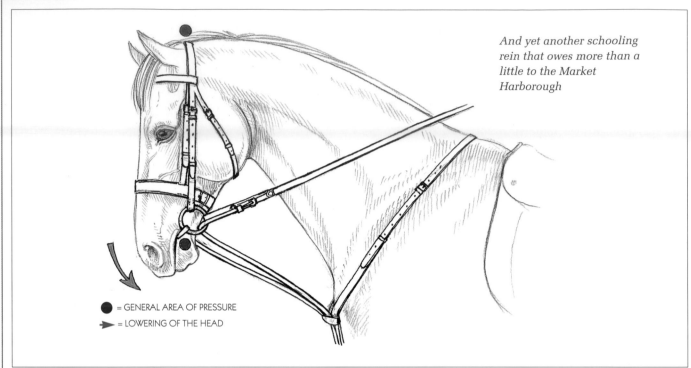

And yet another schooling rein that owes more than a little to the Market Harborough

= GENERAL AREA OF PRESSURE

= LOWERING OF THE HEAD

Everyday use of the rein is made in position (1), when normal schooling can be carried out and the horse jumped over fences up to 3ft 3in (1m) in height. It is claimed that the improved outline will be maintained when the horse is ridden in an ordinary snaffle bridle because of the muscular development which has been induced.

'This patent rein,' claimed its inventor, 'will act as an accelerator, doing in one week what would normally take months of work.'

In the hands of a rider as competent as Peter Abbot-Davies there is no reason not to accept the assertion, but in less experienced hands, accompanied by less than effective legs, there are inherent dangers. The initial position of mouth to tail, in particular, demands an advanced degree of competence or the presence of a skilled trainer supervising from the ground, and those contemplating using the rein would be well advised to take a short course of instruction before embarking on a system that calls for expertise allied to a deep understanding of the theory.

CHAMBON & DE GOGUE

The position of the Chambon and the de Gogue within the category of 'aids to the bit' is not easily defined. In general terms they must belong to the martingale group, whereas in other respects they can be regarded as balancing reins, although that term was never used by their inventors. However, like Abbot-Davies's rein, they are the result of original and logical thinking by very experienced horsemen, and like the Abbot-Davies rein, they have been flattered by imitation.

Both Chambon and de Gogue were French cavalry officers raised in the classical precepts of Saumur but just as influenced by the innovative tradition that belongs uniquely to that school.

It has been held that both reins can legitimately occupy an important, almost integral, place within a progressive system of training; the de Gogue, the more sophisticated and versatile of the two, being both an extension and an expansion of the Chambon. Indeed, its inventor termed it *Système de Gogue* and it is true that the carriage etc. obtained by the device in the exercises from the ground can be maintained and advanced under saddle and in all aspects of general riding, including, in its final position, jumping and cross-country work.

THE CHAMBON

Although the Chambon is not in general use either in Britain or the USA, and its purpose, in consequence, is not always fully understood, it has a very different role in mainland Europe, where it is employed

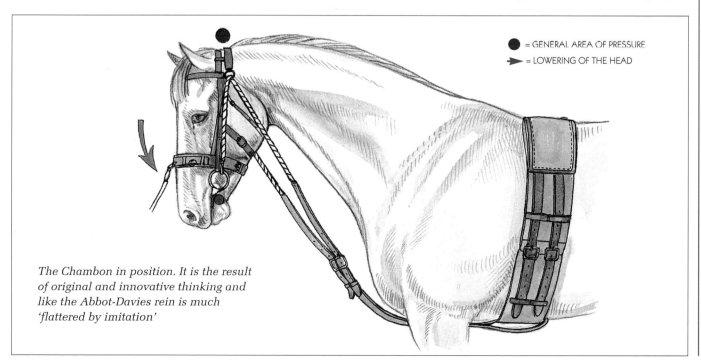

● = GENERAL AREA OF PRESSURE

➤ = LOWERING OF THE HEAD

The Chambon in position. It is the result of original and innovative thinking and like the Abbot-Davies rein is much 'flattered by imitation'

extensively and is often seen as being integral to the lunge equipment.

CONSTRUCTION

The Chambon comprises a felt poll pad fitted with a pulley on either side and fastened over the headpiece of the cavesson or bridle. A leather attachment fastened between the forelegs to a roller or surcingle divides into two branches at the breast. To these branches are attached cords fitted with snap hooks. The cords are passed through the pulleys at the head and are then taken downwards to clip onto the bit rings, the bit being suspended from a light lunge cavesson.

It is preferable to work in a thick rubber or vulcanite mullen-mouth snaffle or one of the flexible plastic ones.

ACTION

The equipment causes a lowering of the head and neck, and in competent hands will result in the shoulders being raised, the back rounded and the hocks engaged more actively under the body. There will be a notable improvement in balance, and the joints of the hip, stifle and hock will be flexed strongly. In time there will be a significant rounded development of the upper muscles of the back and quarters.

The Chambon limits only the upward movement of the head. It does not restrict a lateral movement, nor does it prevent the head being carried forward and downward.

Should the head be thrown upwards in an effort to evade the action it is countered by an *upward* movement of the bit in the mouth, together with a gentle pressure at the nerve centre on the poll. At no time is the restraint imposed a *backward* one that might restrict the stride and so disturb the balance. This seemingly illogical *upward* pressure is central to the Chambon and critical to its action. There is, of course, no risk of the mouth being damaged.

Horses quickly learn to lower the head and work within the frame imposed by the equipment, and without the employment of forceful means. Used consistently with a young horse the Chambon creates a rounded outline which can be maintained by competent riding and occasional reminder lessons in the equipment. It will encourage a rhythmical, balanced movement, and improves immeasurably the flexion of the joints.

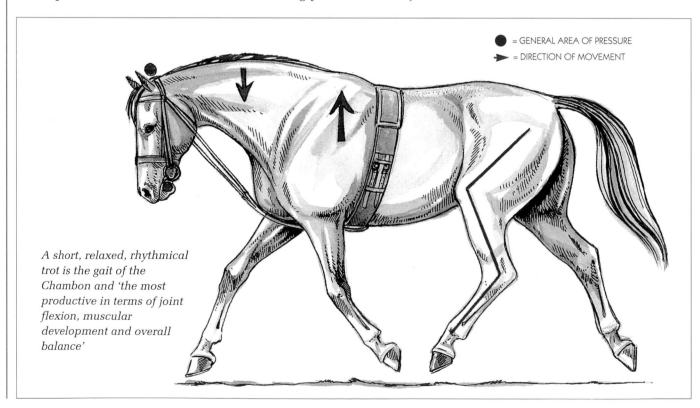

● = GENERAL AREA OF PRESSURE

➤ = DIRECTION OF MOVEMENT

A short, relaxed, rhythmical trot is the gait of the Chambon and 'the most productive in terms of joint flexion, muscular development and overall balance'

Nonetheless, the success of the Chambon, like everything else, depends upon it being used intelligently and upon the trainer insisting always on an energetic, free forward movement originating in active engagement of the hocks. Introductory work carried out correctly and the subsequent adjustment of the cords are particularly important.

METHOD

Initially the horse is worked loose in the training arena with the rein fitted loosely so that it only comes into play as a result of the head being carried, or thrown, excessively high. The cords are then tightened little by little and day by day until the restraint is such that the horse carries *the poll in line with the withers and the nose on a level with the hip bone*. At this point the horse beings to move in the short, relaxed, rhythmical trot that is the gait of the Chambon and the most productive in terms of joint flexion, muscular development and overall balance.

The first lessons should not on any account exceed fifteen minutes in duration otherwise the unaccustomed form and the increased use of the muscles will cause discomfort to the point where the horse is aching in the muscles of the loin and thigh. Nothing, of course, is more likely to cause resentment and resistance.

Once the horse works easily to either hand on the lunge, the training sessions can be increased up to as much as thirty minutes, the equipment being tightened during the last ten minutes to encourage increased use of the back as the horse is sent forward from the whip into the hand. The whip, indeed, is just as essential as the arrangement of the cords. Unless it acts to drive the horse continually forwards into the hand there is no value in the exercise.

On the whole, it is the trot with which the Chambon is most closely associated. The canter is not a gait approaching the trot in terms of making full use of the body and creating muscle. It is not, or should not, be attempted until the trot work is firmly established, and certainly not until the horse has been working in the equipment for upwards of two months.

Because the head is naturally carried somewhat higher in the canter pace, lessons must begin with the rein being adjusted loosely and then tightened by gradual stages until the required outline is obtained.

The Chambon is used only as an adjunct to the lunge exercise, never under saddle.

The words of Anthony Paalman (*Training Showjumpers*) are worth recalling: 'Correct lungeing with the Chambon improves *every* horse. Lungeing is a necessary, as well as an important part of the training of a showjumper. But, regrettably, it does more harm when executed incorrectly. *If the horse is just running around on the lunge, the lungeing is a waste of time.*'

Whilst the Chambon is used with great success in the training of the young horse, it can also be used to advantage in correcting the outline and muscular development of older horses that may have been spoilt by incorrect riding and methods of schooling.

DE GOGUE

Whilst the de Gogue certainly expands and extends the principles implicit in the use of the Chambon, it is far from being just an improved version of the latter. Its inventor called his rein a *system* and it can, indeed, be used in an unbroken progression from the early lessons on the lunge right through the ridden exercises over fences etc. and then in competition.

Although there is a marked similarity between the two reins, the restraints imposed by the de Gogue are more precise and probably more refined, and the apparatus is, obviously, more far-reaching in its effects.

The basis of the de Gogue is the recognition of '*three points of major resistance*' in the unschooled youngster or the badly schooled horse. They are the poll, the mouth and the base of the neck.

To overcome the stiffness caused by resistance in the three areas the rein forms a triangle from the breast to the pulleys on the headpiece, through the bit rings and thence back again to the chest. Within the confines of the triangle the horse learns to carry the head comfortably in the lowered position dictated by the adjustment.

AIDS TO THE BIT

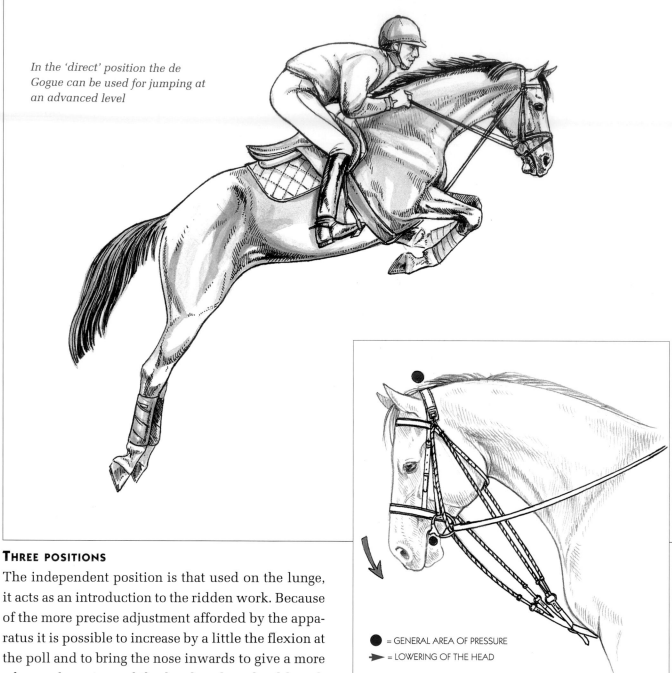

In the 'direct' position the de Gogue can be used for jumping at an advanced level

The de Gogue in its 'independent' position with the addition of a riding rein

● = GENERAL AREA OF PRESSURE
➤ = LOWERING OF THE HEAD

THREE POSITIONS

The independent position is that used on the lunge, it acts as an introduction to the ridden work. Because of the more precise adjustment afforded by the apparatus it is possible to increase by a little the flexion at the poll and to bring the nose inwards to give a more advanced carriage of the head and neck, although this must be approached by gradual stages and cannot be attempted without free, energetic movement.

The risk of the horse becoming overbent is obviated by 'stops' fitted to the rein below the small pulley on the poll pad.

The next stage is to attach an ordinary rein to the bit ring with the apparatus in the same independent position and retaining the 'triangle of constraint'. With the addition of the rein the training can be con-

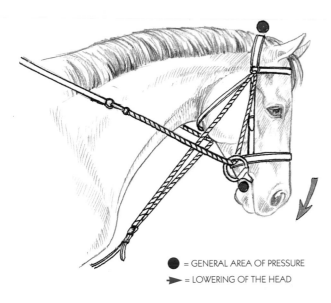

● = GENERAL AREA OF PRESSURE

➤ = LOWERING OF THE HEAD

Detail of the de Gogue in the 'direct' position. The system is not for the novice rider

Below: The de Gogue fitted for the lunge exercises. The diagram shows clearly the triangle of the three points of resistance

tinued from the saddle, although initially the rein should be loosened until the horse is accustomed to the weight on its back and answers to the leg aids.

The third position is termed 'direct', the triangle being completed by the rein going directly to the hand. It is possible to fix an additional rein so that the de Gogue can be operated temporarily on the principle of the draw rein, and this is probably advisable for all save the most experienced riders; it also, of course, acts as an introduction to the use of the direct rein.

In the direct position the horse can be ridden across country and over arena fences, the rider, it is claimed, obtaining maximum control with the minimum of effort, the horse responding smoothly to the action of the hand and performing with all the athleticism of which it is capable.

Without doubt, the de Gogue has an appeal for the dedicated rider. Unfortunately, that appeal may be shared by the less-than-competent. Like so many of these ingenious schooling reins, the de Gogue does not come within the province of the novice, and even riders at a higher level should use it only under the supervision of an experienced instructor.

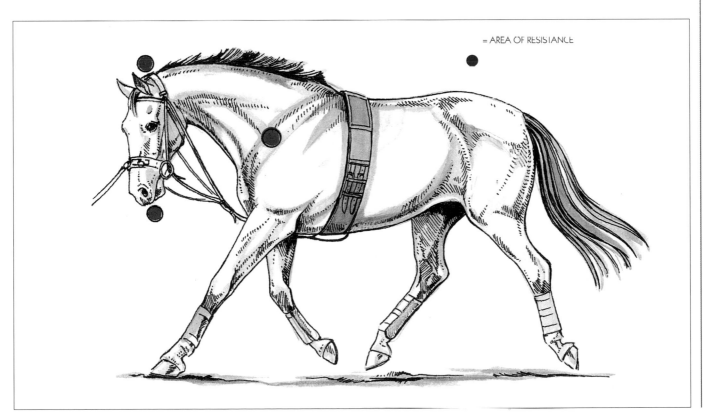

● = AREA OF RESISTANCE

COMMON EVASIONS

The horse is able to produce a remarkable number of evasions to the action of the bit. Some arise from conformational defects in the mouth, but most are the fault of incorrect early training or an ill-fitting, or carelessly adjusted, bridle.

The most common problem is that of getting the tongue over the bit. This occurs when the tongue is drawn back and then clamped over the top of the mouthpiece. It reduces the rider's control by an alarming degree. In extreme instances the tongue may be drawn back so far as to block the larynx, when the condition is described as 'swallowing' the tongue and there is a risk of choking. In any event the horse comes to a sudden stop.

A 'soft palate' may predispose a horse to retract its tongue. A shallow tongue channel may be the cause of the tongue being damaged by bit pressure, or it may otherwise become bruised or pinched so that the discomfort experienced causes evasion. Most often the habit – and the trick of laying the tongue over the bit soon becomes habitual – is the result of careless bitting combined with a disregard of the simplest principles involved, or, more usually, a complete ignorance of them. Too large a jointed snaffle, or one adjusted too low in the mouth, is an invitation to the horse to avoid the discomfort by putting his tongue firmly over the mouthpiece. The first action to be taken to correct the evasion is to remove the jointed snaffle and replace it with a simple mullen mouthpiece adjusted sufficiently high in the mouth. Very often the change alone will provide an immediate solution; if not, further measures will be necessary.

An old remedy is the rubber **juba port** which can be fastened round a mullen mouthpiece so that it is pointing to the rear and lies over the tongue. Bits can be made with a central tongue grid and are usually effective so long as the bit fits snugly to the cheeks. A **tongue grid** suspended in the mouth above the bit provides another solution but is something of a mouthful.

There is then a piece of equipment which used to be known as a **T.O.B. device**. It was made of two

The Juba port used with a mullen mouthpiece to counteract the habit of laying the tongue over the bit

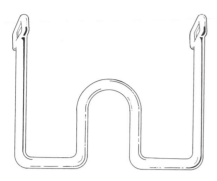

A tongue grid suspended in the mouth is an effective deterrent to the horse inclined to put his tongue over the bit

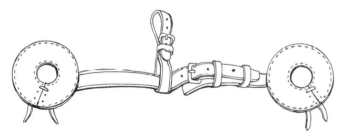

A clever T.O.B. device which raises the bit in the mouth and also puts a restraint on the nose

A tongue plate is incorporated into the mouthpiece of this bit to keep the tongue in place

circular pieces of stout leather fitted to either end of a mullen mouthpiece and connected by an adjustable strap. The device raises the bit in the mouth, a prerequisite in these cases, but also places a little pressure on the nose which is probably an additional help in countering the problem.

In the racing industry, not noted for its appreciation of the niceties of bitting, the Draconian deterrent of the tongue strap adjusted tightly round the lower jaw is sometimes employed. Of course, it prevents the tongue from being moved at all, and for the short period it is worn, which should be no more than the duration of the race, it can be effective. Conversely, there are horses which strongly resent its presence, and in those circumstances it will do more harm than good.

Far more acceptable is the rubber **Australian cheeker** which not only lifts the bit in the mouth but acts to increase the control through the psychological restraint induced by the central part of the cheeker running straight up the face.

The Australian cheeker lifts the bit in the mouth as well as exerting a psychological restraint. It is much used in racing on the flat or over fences

STRAIGHTENING BITS

These bits are within the province of the racecourse and are used to counter the difficulties caused by the horse that is 'one-sided' in the mouth, hangs persistently to one side or another or, in steeplechasing, has developed the knack of running down the fence to the embarrassment of its jockey and the exasperation, succinctly expressed, of his colleagues.

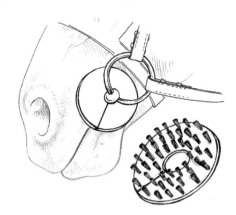

A brush pricker acts as a gentle reminder to run straight without hanging to one side or the other

A **brush pricker** used on whatever side was needed was once a popular remedy for the horse that would not run straight. Initially it works, but horses can get so used to it that its effect is lost.

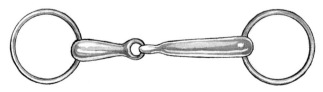

The anti-lug bit used to counteract the horse that hangs to one side

An **anti-lug** bit a jointed snaffle with one side of the mouthpiece shorter than the other, can be of some help, the sharply curved short side being fitted on the opposite side to that on which the horse hangs.

The squeezing action of a **circle cheek** bit, or, indeed, any snaffle fitted with large rings or even cheeks, helps to keep horses running straight, but they must fit snugly so that they cannot slide across the mouth.

The Americans, who have some sharply cornered

The circle-cheek snaffle, if fitted snugly, helps to keep a horse running straight

tracks and are consequently particularly conscious of steerage problems, have a variety of ingenious designs, some of them borrowed from the harness racers.

The nosenet. An example of the intelligent application of psychology

PULLERS

Of course, there are all sorts of 'strong' bits, many of which have been discussed previously, but as good a remedy as any for the confirmed tearaway, and one that causes no pain, is the **nosenet** fastened by small straps over the muzzle. Admittedly there is a slight pressure on the tender muzzle, but it is the very fact that the net is there that causes the horse to draw back from it. The effect is almost entirely psychological, but it works.

Cab-horses in the days when they were recruited from the hard-mouthed cast-offs of the racecourse were often fitted with a nosenet in the very real interests of control in crowded city streets.

Part VI

SPECIALIST BITTING

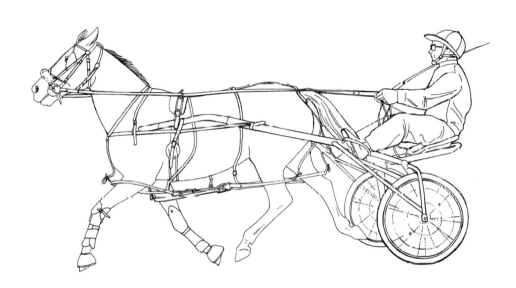

SPECIALIST BITTING

POLO

Polo is the fastest game in the world and enormously demanding of pony and rider in terms of split-second reactions. It goes without saying that balance is essential in both members of the partnership, but instant control at high speeds is just as paramount a factor.

Traditionally, the polo pony was mouthed and bitted with great exactitude and attention to detail. A pony that was uncomfortable in the mouth or had suffered damage as a result of the bit soon lost heart and interest for the game.

In the great days of polo, a decade or more before World War I and up to World War II, the bitting of the polo pony relied predominantly on the double bridle and the Pelham, both bit and curb chain being fitted with absolute precision and then supported by a standing martingale that was just as carefully adjusted. Thereafter, with a new equitational philosophy and another generation, the tendency was towards the employment of the large ring gag used in conjunction with the standing martingale and on occasions with a number of additional restraints as well. Side-reins were, and are, frequently included in the equipment, along with noseband attachments that keep the mouth closed. Just occasionally a pony is fitted with the unpleasantly strong and potentially damaging rope noseband as a further means of restraint.

Add these items to a gag operating against the standing martingale on the noseband and one has the most powerful bitting arrangement in the world.

Possibly it is something of a kitchen-sink approach and it certainly lacks the niceties of the meticulously fitted double or Pelham bridle, on the other hand it

Despite, or perhaps because of, a bitting arrangement comprising gag, running rein, martingale, hosal and drop-noseband, this polo pony accepts the situation without resentment

can be argued that the potential to damage a mouth is not as great as that of a double bridle. Additional weight is given to that view when one appreciates that the majority of present-day riders are decidedly snaffle-orientated and that a great many have never ridden in anything else.

The only variation to the stoutly made martingale, which for preference and convenience adjusts at breast height, is the Indian **puggaree** martingale ie a turban looped at the girth end and tied to the noseband at the other. It is colourful and attractive, but more importantly it has that bit of stretch not found in the leather martingale.

Sometimes a polo pony may be fitted with a nosenet, as described in the previous chapter. Possibly it is there as part of the armoury of control, but it is just as likely to have been put on to prevent the pony biting his companions.

Left: The exercise in ultimate control or ultimate over kill

171

SPECIALIST BITTING

DRIVING

At the turn of the nineteenth century when the streets of the world's principal cities were choked with every sort of horse-drawn vehicle the variety of driving bits was enormous, far exceeding the number of riding bits. In 1890 in London alone there was a horse population of over 300,000, almost all of which worked in draught, whilst a small American town like Milwaukee, population 350,000, supported 12,500 horses.

Today the choice of a driving bit is far more limited and is really centred round three basic patterns: the four-ring **Wilson snaffle**, the **Liverpool** and the **Buxton**, the last two offering a number of variations in their construction.

The **Wilson** is attached to the bridle head by the loose inside ring, the reins being fastened round *both* rings, when the action is a mild one. The action becomes more severe if the reins are buckled only to the outside bit rings, because the nutcracker effect is then intensified and there is a strong squeezing pressure against the jaws.

The Wilson ring driving snaffle – not sophisticated but not impractical

The **Liverpool** bit is made in various forms and offers up to five positions (if the cheek is made with three rein slots) for the attachment of the reins. Mouthpieces are usually straight-bar, smooth on one side and rough on the other so that the bit can be made more or less severe. Liverpool bits may have either a slide cheek or a fixed cheek, this latter being favoured when driving a pair. One prominent German loriner offers the Liverpool bit with a ported mouth and also includes a mild butterfly cheek in the range.

The rein positions possible are: (1) *plain cheek*, which acts just as the snaffle mouthpiece; (2) *rough*

The Liverpool driving bit offers a variety of rein fittings and is probably the bit in most general use

Liverpool rein positions
1 *Plain cheek*
2 *Rough cheek*
3 *Middle bar*
4 *Bottom bar*

A rose by any other name ... the Elbow bit is no more than the Army Universal and none the worse for that, but it would be better with a bar connecting the cheeks at their extremities

cheek, giving a little curb action; (3) *middle bar*, producing more curb action; and (4) *bottom bar*, giving strong curb action. However, the latter is rarely employed. If the bit is made with three rein slots in the cheek there will be the addition of the *upper bar*, giving curb action between that of the rough cheek position and the middle bar fastening.

A further variation on the Liverpool is the **elbow Bit**, in which the cheeks are set back at an angle to prevent the horse taking hold of them with its teeth. It offers the same number of rein positions.

PAIR HARNESS

For sporting vehicles the Liverpool is considered suitable, but it needs to have a connecting bar between the bottom of the cheeks to prevent them from being caught up in the coupling reins or in the bridle of the pair horse, and it is better if the cheek is of the fixed type.

The formal Buxton bit offers a number of rein positions. Mouthpieces vary but there is always a crossbar to prevent a rein being caught up between the cheeks

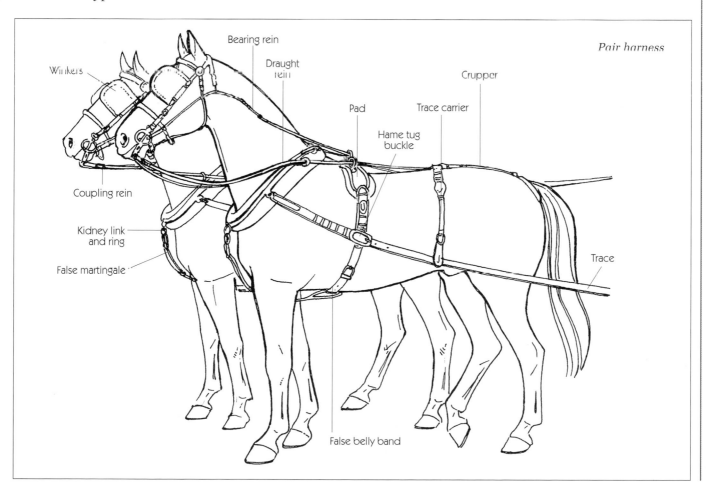

Pair harness

Winkers

Bearing rein

Draught rein

Crupper

Pad

Trace carrier

Hame tug buckle

Coupling rein

Kidney link and ring

False martingale

Trace

False belly band

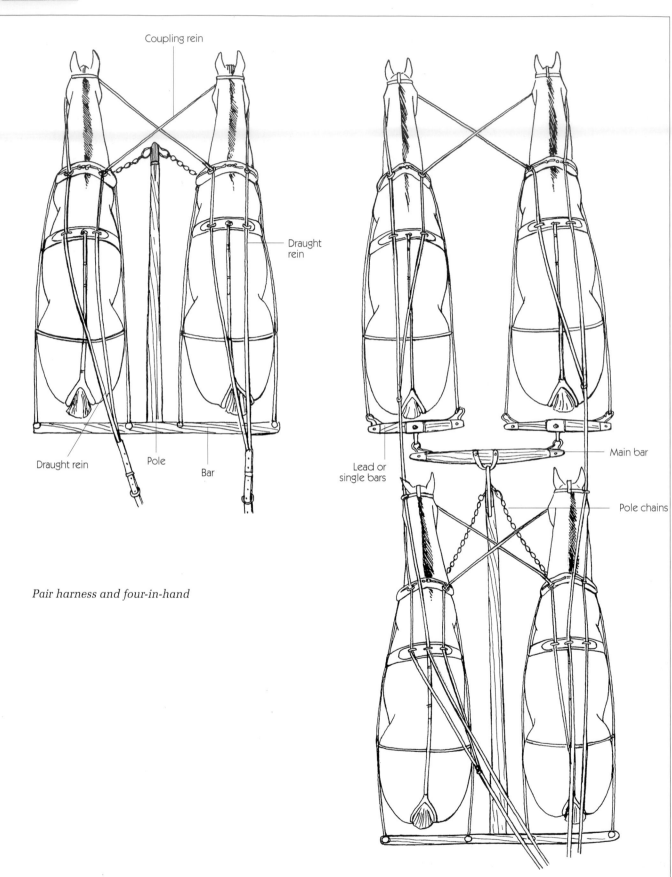

Coupling rein

Draught rein

Draught rein

Pole

Bar

Pair harness and four-in-hand

Lead or single bars

Main bar

Pole chains

On the more formal turnout the more ornate **Buxton** bit is preferred. The action is much the same as that of the Liverpool, and the curved cheeks are always joined at the bottom by a crossbar. Mouthpieces in the Buxton vary from a number of ported mouths to the plain straight bar.

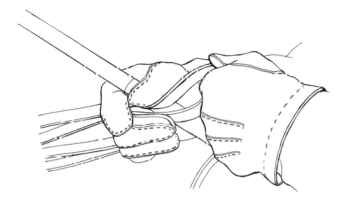

Method of holding the reins when driving a four-in-hand

Pair harness (and team harness, too) requires the addition of a *coupling rein*. There are two 'draught' reins from the outside of the bits to the whip's (driver's) hand, and two coupling reins buckled to the draught reins some 24in (61cm) from the hand: one is fastened to the left of the off-side horse's bit, and the other that is attached to the right draught rein is fastened to the right side of the near-side horse's bit. It follows that when the left rein is pulled both horses turn to the left, and vice versa.

The exact adjustment of the coupling reins is a critical factor in pair driving, the aim being to have both horses moving with their heads held straight to the front. If the reins are too long, contact is on the outside of the horses' mouths via the draught reins; if too short, then the horses' heads will be bent inwards.

Bearing reins are an artificial means of raising the head carriage. They are not much seen in Britain but are still incorporated in some American types of harness. There are two types, both involving a bradoon fitted above the driving bit. One operates on a pulley and the other is attached directly to the bradoon.

HARNESS RACING

Harness racing bits reflect the sport's prime requirement for the horse to run carrying the head straight to the front. It is, indeed, very essential that the requirement is observed, since a horse holding the head to one side or another will not be able to produce the maximum speed of which it is capable, and will also run the very real risk of striking into itself and sustaining serious injury when travelling at speeds between 30 and 40mph (48 and 64 kmph).

The basic driving bridle is an 'open' one – that is, not fitted with blinkers (visors) – but blinkers are, nonetheless, in pretty general use on the harness raceways to encourage the horse to look immediately to his front. Horses that persistently carry the head to one side may be fitted with a **Murphy blind**, the invention of the notable American trainer and driver Thomas W. Murphy. The stiff leather blind is shaped inwards slightly in front of the eye. With a horse which turns the head to the left, the blind is fitted on the right so that it covers the eye when the head is carried too far to the side. The opposite fitting deals with the horse attempting to bend the neck to the right.

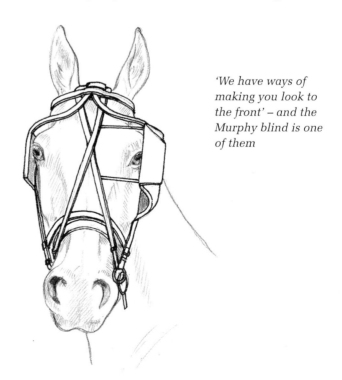

'We have ways of making you look to the front' – and the Murphy blind is one of them

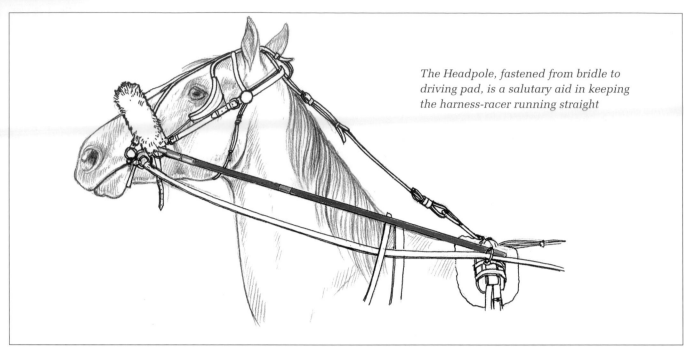

The Headpole, fastened from bridle to driving pad, is a salutary aid in keeping the harness-racer running straight

Another straightening device is the **head pole**, running from the noseband to the driving saddle alongside the neck and head. The poles are telescopically adjustable to whatever length is required. To reinforce the action of the pole it can be fitted with a ball or a burr, a length of leather studded with blunt rivets, where it comes in contact with the neck.

Harness racing bits, disregarding those designed specifically to discourage the head-benders, are either jointed or straight-bar and are made to fit very closely, most patterns having cheeks to prevent any possibility of their not remaining absolutely central in the mouth. To assist the snug fit still further, use is also made of a chin strap.

There are very many ingenious bit patterns to cope with the horse which persists in leaning to one

Slide mouth bit to counteract any tendency to lean to one side

Frisco June. A close-fitting, comfortable bit with a chin strap that is suitable for young horses

| *Simple, rubber-covered, spoon cheek harness bit*

The 'Side-liner', a form of correction for horses tending to veer to one side or the other

The Shadow Roll noseband is a deterrent against shying and an aid to concentration

side. A popular one is the **side-liner**, which has an extension to the mouthpiece protruding to one side fitted at its end with a ring to which the rein can be attached. Obviously, this arrangement gives an extra leverage which may well be enough to keep the head straight.

An additional aid in harness racing is the **shadow roll**, much demeaned in Europe by being termed 'sheepskin noseband'. These are seen not infrequently in flat-racing both in Europe and America, but they belong firmly to the sport of harness racing which, of necessity, pays far more attention to its equipment.

There are a number of shadow roll patterns, some of them extending upwards to above the eye, but the object remains the same. They are fitted with great care so that the harness horse can see straight ahead, which is essential, but cannot look downwards at the ground in front. Its use is in countering any tendency to shy at shadows, marks on the track and so on. Pacers – that is harness racers employing the lateral 'pacing' action rather than the conventional diagonal trotting gait – are probably more likely to spook than the trotting horse. Possibly this is because pacers wear hobbles round the legs to prevent their breaking the gait, and because of the restriction they appear to be more concerned about tripping and the ground underfoot and can react violently at real or imagined objects on the ground. In a situation where a dozen horses are moving in close proximity at high speed a shying horse is just not an option.

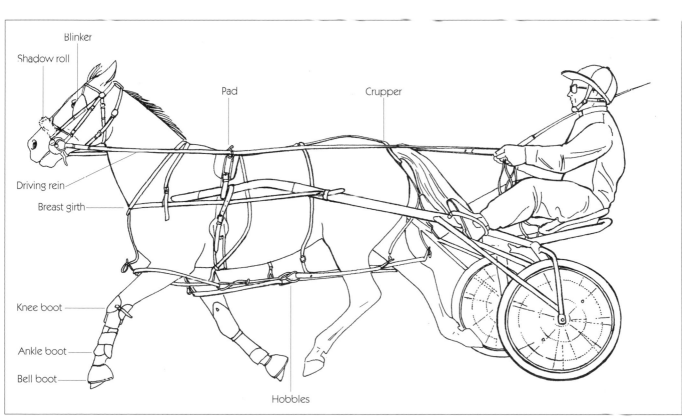

Blinker
Shadow roll
Pad
Crupper
Driving rein
Breast girth
Knee boot
Ankle boot
Bell boot
Hobbles

The fearsome Raymond over-check, kept in place with either a chinstrap or a curb chain, operates powerfully on the nose

A plain, standard overcheck used in conjunction with the harness bit

The straight-bar Speedway overcheck

PULLING

The other problem with the harness-racer, either pacer or trotter, is the inclination to pull rather too strongly when excited. To counter the tearaway, or at least to keep the strong-pulling horse within reasonable bounds, there are all sorts of ingeniously contrived devices. The principal amongst these is the **overcheck** bit, or the more common overcheck rein. The overcheck bit is just a thin snaffle with small rings fitted above the driving bit. The reins are fastened to both and certainly increase the control, but not to the extent possible with the overcheck rein. This runs from the extra check bit up the face and then through pulleys or rings on the bridle head, passing to the rear from that point to fasten to the driving saddle.

Indeed, straps that cross the face are a feature of the harness racing bridle and are themselves a form of restraint (shades of those Assyrian horsemen and their strong-necked horses of 2000 years past.)

The check rein gives considerably more control to the driver and it also prevents the horse from pulling down the head in moments of excitement, at the start, for instance, an action that has to be discouraged as something of a priority.

The ultimate deterrent has to be the **lip cord**, a device that might reasonably be thought barbaric and is likely to prove counter-productive in consequence. It is a cord fastened around the top gums under the upper lip. It lies behind the bit's mouthpiece and emerges at the corners of the mouth, to be fastened, one presumes pretty tightly, under the chin.

Part VII

METALS AND MATERIALS

METALS AND MATERIALS

Ever since horsemen began to appreciate that comfort in the horse's mouth led to increased salivation and an accompanying relaxation, efforts have been made to provide a mouthpiece to the bit that would be an encouragement to these desirable ends.

Long, long ago copper was a favourite material for bit-making, particularly in Mexico and South America. For centuries, iron bits have been made on the Iberian Peninsula, and are everywhere apparent in modern Spain and Portugal. Today, iron is presented as something of a panacea to the problems of the mouth and marketed accordingly, and so, of course, is copper.

It could be that in times past copper and iron were the most easily available materials and were used on that account alone. It would, for instance, be hard to imagine the Celts, the ironworkers of the day who invented the curb bit and the horseshoe, being much concerned with flexions of the lower jaw.

Much later rubber and vulcanite were incorporated into the loriner's craft and were hailed as being soft in the mouth and mild in their action, which may well be true. There was a breaking snaffle and a famous Pelham, the Kerro, with a wooden mouthpiece (necessarily, of hard *lignum vitae*) both of which were hailed as positive encouragements to 'making the mouth'.

In about the same period, leather mouthpieces (in effect, a piece of rawhide sewn around a steel mouthpiece) were in favour, and many horsemen of that era wrapped a mouthing bit for a youngster in a bandage soaked, very messily, in syrup.

Today, bits are made largely from stainless steel and often in far-off places where horses are hardly a

Copper

Copper and steel

Stainless steel

Sweet iron

Leather

part of day-to-day life, but there are also progressive companies marketing bits of 'high-tech alloy' – that is, 'nickel-free' and containing a significant element of copper – as well as one, a most prestigious German company, that sells 'oxidised' bits which are patented under a brand name.

Additionally, and very importantly, there are ranges of flexible polyurethane plastic mouthpieces, successors to the vulcanite and rubber bits, which conform very well to the shape of the individual mouth; and, in one case, they have even introduced an apple flavour. The products of these companies are *very* good, but the claims made for them are in many instances nothing short of monstrous, and impossible to substantiate.

Nickel, once euphemistically titled 'solid nickel', was rustless and cheap, otherwise it had nothing to commend it. It would bend and break, and it turned a disgusting yellow colour. Thirty years ago I wrote that 'I would neither use it nor recommend it' and I never have. The named nickel mixtures like Eglantine, Kangaroo and Premier were an altogether different kettle of fish and thoroughly reliable in all respects. Whether these bits were responsible for 'nickel allergies', which one 'golden metal' company claims are more and more prevalent nowadays, is a matter on which I am not qualified to comment. I have no experience of a 'nickel allergy', nor do I know that these golden, oxidised metals 'produce the distinctive and pleasant taste that horses love. This particular taste encourages horses to chew and produce saliva which promotes rapid acceptance...'

Perhaps it does, but there is no scientific evidence to prove the claim and it is very unlikely that there ever will be. Has anyone, one wonders, consulted the horse?

If we believe our horses are more comfortable, happier and go better in a bit made of one material or another, that is a sufficient reason for using it, so long as one is sure that the construction is suitable.

On the other hand we might reflect on the old horseman's saying: 'T'aint so much what you put in 'is mouth as the 'ands at the end of the rein.'

Rubber

Rubber-covered or vulcanite

Polyurethane (Happy Mouth)

INDEX

INDEX

INDEX

AUTHOR'S ACKNOWLEDGEMENTS

My thanks are due to my illustrator Maggie Raynor, an old friend, for her singular contribution to the book; to the directors of Buxactic Ltd for their help and co-operation in providing illustrations of the Sprenger bit range; to my long-suffering literary agent, John Pawsey, for his patience, encouragement and unfailing support and to Julie Thomas for her expert collation and presentation of my manuscript. Finally I have to thank my wife who puts up with me.

The publishers would like to thank Buxactic Ltd, Abbey Saddlery and Crafts Ltd and Saddlery Trade Services (distributor of the Happy Mouth range) for supplying photographs of the bits and the following for providing other illustrative material:
Michael Holford: pp2–3(British Museum), 9(Turkish National Museum), 12–13, 16, 18–9, 20btm, 23 and 25(all British Museum), 29(Musée de Bayeux)
C.M. Dixon: pp4–5 (British Library), 6, 26 (British Museum), 27top (Istanbul Archaeological Museum), 27btm (National Archaeological Museum of Rome)
Robert Harding Picture Library: p7
Tony Stone Images: p8(Photo: Paul Harris)
Mary Evans Picture Library: pp10, 11, 21btm, 24top, 34top
H Mäder: p14
Katz Pictures: pp15 & 22 (Mansell/Time Inc)
Kit Houghton: pp22, 32top, 52, 71, 72–3, 75, 81left, 86, 93, 95, 99, 100, 102, 128, 131btm left, 134, 135, 137, 139top&btm rt, 140rt, 142rt, 143, 144btm rt, 145, 147, 158btm, 167btm rt, 170, 171
Frank Spooner Pictures: p33 ©Gamma/Photo by Jean-Luc Petit
The Bridgeman Art Library: p36top (Collection of the Earl of Pembroke, Wilton House, Wilts, UK)
V&A Picture Library: p36btm
Author's collection: pp37, 41
Werner Menzendorf: p38
Bob Langrish: pp105, 106, 109, 177top
Dr Derek Knottenbelt, University of Liverpool Department of Veterinary Clinical Science & Animal Husbandry: p117left

All line artworks by Maggie Raynor except pp70btm, 81top rt, 107left, 122, 123, 167top left by Sally Alexander